Open Windows
- Remediation Strategies in Global Film Adaptations

Open Windows
- Remediation Strategies in Global Film Adaptations

Edited by Kyle Nicholas & Jørgen Riber Christensen

Aalborg University Press

Open Windows
- Remediation Strategies in Global Film Adaptation
Edited by:
Kyle Nicholas & Jørgen Riber Christensen

© The Authors and Aalborg University Press, 2005

Cover: Torben Lundsted
Layout: Lars Pedersen, Anblik
Printed by Narayana Press
ISBN 87-7307-742-9

Distribution:
Aalborg University Press
Niels Jernes Vej 6B
9220 Aalborg Ø
Denmark
Phone: (+45) 96 35 71 40, Fax (+45) 96 35 00 76
E-mail: aauf@forlag.aau.dk
Homepage: http://www.forlag.aau.dk

All rights reserved. No part of this book may be reprinted or reproduced or utilized in any form or by any electronic, mechanical, or other means, now known or hereafter invented, including photocopying and recording, or in any information storage or retrieval system, without permission in writing from the publishers, except for reviews and short excerpts in scholarly publications.

This book is published with financial support of Department of Communication and Department of Languages and International Cultural Studies, Aalborg University, Denmark and with financial support of Old Dominion University, Norfolk, VA, USA.

The CD-ROM

System Requirements:
Win 98/Me/2000/XP
8x speed cd-rom drive
A Pentium processor-based PC or compatible computer
At least 128MB of RAM
3 Megabytes of free hard disk plus 11 MB for QuickTime
Sound card
At least QuickTime 6.5 (part of the cd-rom's installation)
The display area of the screen must be set to 1024 x 768 and to High Color (16 bits)
The cd-rom must stay in the drive when the program is being used.

Installation:
Insert the cd-rom in your cd-rom drive. Click on "Start" on the Windows screen, choose "Run", and then type: d:\setup.exe. If your cd-rom drive has been assigned another letter than d, you must type this letter instead of d. At the end of the installation you are asked if you want to install QuickTime. If you do not have QuickTime 6.5 on your computer, or if you do not know whether you have or not, choose "Yes". If you later discover that you should have installed QuickTime, the easiest thing is to repeat the whole installation. The installation program may pause if your system does not meet the requirements of the program. You can select the right display area and number of colours by clicking with the right mouse button on your desktop and then choose Properties. When the installation is completed, an icon appears on your desktop. You start the program by double-clicking on it. The program may also be started form Window's Program start. The cd-rom must be in the drive.

The program can be removed in Window's Control panel.

Set-up of the QuickTime Player:
On some computers the default preferences of the QuickTime player may cause some problems. Especially on older computers it is recommended that the default settings are modified after the installation of QuickTime. It is done in this way:
Open the Quick Time players by clicking on its icon on the desktop or through Window's Programs. In the Quick Time player choose Edit > Preferences > Quick Time Preferences. In the scroll window at the top choose "Video settings" and then "Safe Mode (GDI only)".

The problems that are prevented are:
When a new video clip is played the old video image covers it.
The video clips are played with sound but black image.
The program freezes if the sound volume is changed when a video clip is playing.

Contents

Preface	9
Introduction *Kyle Nicholas*	11
Dig that Cowboy – Textual Networks in the Adaptation Process *Kyle Nicholas*	23
Remediation Made Fun – Examining the Dynamics of Comic and Computer Game Tie-ins *Torben Poulsen*	35
Adaptation in *Adaptation* – A Real Fictitious Story(line) *Bent Sørensen*	59
Adapting Emotions in *The Hours* *Steen Christiansen*	79
***Medea* Re-mediated** *Ove Christensen*	97
Found in Translation Domestic-Universal Strategy in Adapting *Babette's Feast* *Gunhild Agger*	117
Dickens Adaptations from *South Park* to *Futurama* *Jørgen Riber Christensen*	139
Teening Shakespeare *Michael Skovmand*	157
Index	173

Preface

This book is the result of a long collaborative process that sprung from a faculty exchange program between Aalborg University in Denmark and Old Dominion University in the USA. Although these exchanges had been going on for several years, conditions in the spring of 2004 seemed ripe for an exploration of different viewpoints on the adaptation of films. The struggle for the acceptance of film criticism and history in academe – both in Europe and in the United States – is a long one. This book is in part a celebration of the burgeoning popularity of media studies in European and American universities, as well as a call to expand our critique in an era of emerging digital media. Those new media, particularly email and the web, were critical tools in crafting this volume, as the editors used the web to post drafts and email to exchange dozens (and dozens) comments, critiques, and questions, as well as the midnight worries endemic to a transatlantic enterprise of this nature. But, the creative spark was initiated in the face-to-face conversations between authors and editors, and for those opportunities, and so much more, we have some people to thank.

Special thanks to Janeen Smith Jørgensen, International Coordinator in the Faculty of Humanities at Aalborg University. Janeen's assistance in arranging for visits to and from Aalborg and Old Dominion was invaluable, as was her early enthusiasm for this project. At Old Dominion, Steve Johnson and John Heyl, from the Dragas International Center, have opened doors for many faculty and students and their assistance with the scholar exchange program is much appreciated. Chandra de Silva, Dean of the College of Arts and Letters, and Annette Finley-Croswhite, Associate Dean, were instrumental in securing the time and funding to make this book a reality. Many thanks are also due to the faculty of the Communication and Theatre Arts Department at Old Dominion University for their support of this long undertaking. At Aalborg University we thank Torben Vestergaard, Head of the Department of Languages and Intercultural Studies and Christian Jantzen, Head of the Department of Communication for their financial support and encouragement.

The scholarly life has many charms, but the sustained concentration that makes a volume like this possible can take its toll on our loved ones. For their patience and constant love we thank Tarina and Jane.

Kyle Nicholas
Jørgen Riber Christensen
30 October 2005

Introduction

Kyle Nicholas

A camera, a café and a train

George Méliès was sitting in the basement of the Grand Café when a train steamed into the room: 'At this sight, we sat with our mouths open, thunderstruck, speechless with amazement. At the end of the screening, all was madness, and everyone wanted to know how they might obtain the same results' (Putnam 2000 p.11). The apocryphal story of cinema's birth is suitably one of technology, space and spectacle. The Lumière brothers, technicians and capitalists of the first order, gathered about 30 paying customers into the Salon Indien and proceeded to awe them with a technological achievement when they 'saw' a train pull into La Ciotat Station.

The industrial overtones of that day in Paris cannot be mistaken. The Lumières had been instructed by their father to perfect a marketable film technology (their debut was a meeting of the Society for Encouragement of National Industry). The train itself was an icon of industrialization in an era where transportation and communication had only recently been separated. The *cinematographe* was a camera, printer and projector all in one. Viewers were impressed by the large, clattering, hand-cranked apparatus in the center of the room that spewed the steaming locomotive into their laps. Méliès was transformed by that day in 1895.

A magician and amateur filmmaker, Méliès was ordering custom built cameras within a couple of months. But while others were perfecting the single shot film, Méliès was working his magic within the camera, manipulating multiple exposures into 'trick' films. He later established much of early film language. His technique culminated in *A Trip to the Moon* (1902) which demonstrated his dexterity in layering images, editing shots, and stringing together a believable narrative from single-shot scenes. Méliès' cinematographic sleight-of-hand (and the century of film that followed) evokes the same cognitive and emotional reactions of any fine magical performance: viewers simultaneously observe the process and are drawn into it. While identifying with the performers, we cannot help but marvel at the technique and ask ourselves: How does he do it?

This volume is an exploration of that nexus of story and form – of narrative, technique and industrial practices – embodied in media adaptations. The focus here is on media that have been adapted into films, but we reject the notion that the filmic form is final or that the source text is primal. Rather, we look at film adaptation as part of an ongoing process of repurposing and rearticulation. The films are single stars in a constellation of form and meaning. Like the radiance of stars, the qualities of any particular textual iteration are refracted through time and space. Our location, cognitively, perceptually and physically, shifts our understanding of both the endogenous and exogenous particulars of texts. In other words, our perceptions of what a film is really saying and its relevance depend a great deal upon where we sit and when and how we watch. Beyond time and space, our view (and here we exhaust the utility of our analogy) is conditioned by the lens we employ.

The digital age in which we live foregrounds the socio-industrial complex of technologies that shapes our media experiences. We see the explosion of technology not only in international blockbusters like *Titanic* (1997), and the *Harry Potter* and *Lord of the Rings* series, but also in the trend toward digital cameras and computer editing, and especially in the repurposing of texts into digital products. Digital technologies infiltrate not only production but reception. Of the top 20 grossing films of all time, 19 are special effects bonanzas (*The Passion of the Christ*, 2004, may be the singular exception, depending on how one interprets the meaning of 'special effects'). If audiences have come to expect the impossible in film, courtesy of digital effects, they also expect the rapid remediation of films into the panoply of digital transmutations that circulate our multitudinous communication channels. In our digital age films comprise a kind of databank as their 'long-heralded specificity now seems to be dissolving into the larger bitstream of the audiovisual media' (Stam 2005, p.12). Once digitized, films can be fragmented, their various parts plugged into new contexts, their stories stripped or altered, their images relocated in a hyper-pastiche that both extends and threatens the industrial practices of their inception and the artistic vision of their creators. Filmmakers become ambi-reflexive, not only incorporating and commenting upon anterior texts, but anticipating the reinscription of their own productions. And so film scholars must expand their toolsets and their visions to accommodate these processes. The authors in this volume illustrate multi-perspectival, metatheoretical approaches to film adaptation. Each chapter explores the conjunction of multiple texts in a unique way. The next few paragraphs lay out some of the common assumptions and understandings that bond the volume as a whole.

Open Windows

In keeping with the theme of this volume, the title, *Open Windows*, is meant to invite the reader in, to join us in making sense of the film adaptations discussed in these pages. The term 'open' has various meanings for media scholars. We would not think of defining the term too precisely (and thus closing off interaction in the very act of opening up to it), but a few thoughts on the subject will be helpful. First, we can think of open in terms of audience power in making meaning. In this sense, all texts are open as all texts are subject to the cultural predilections and cognitive processes of understanding. Audiences read into and through books, films and other media, selectively decoding textual signs in a more or less idiosyncratic process. Interpretation is a creative activity that transpires between an author and her various readers. To that extent every text is open because it automatically embodies multiple meanings that are selected, crafted and asserted by readers (or audiences). Texts, particularly in our digital age, are unfinished artifacts. Fans' ability to add to or delete from digitized texts, to recontextualize images and rework plotlines represents second type of openness. Novels, films, videogames, and comic books are all subject to new processes of mixing, morphing and other manipulations.

While the commercial repurposing of texts is a primary focus of this volume, we are cognizant of the myriad ways in which adaptations are quickly re-adapted and remediated by a profusion of quasi-authors across a spectrum of digital media. Each of these new versions reflects back on and potentially alters perceptions of the earlier text. The concept of open text takes on a third meaning in sectors of the online world, where it borrows an idea from the open source software movement. Open source advocates distribute their software to a community that is free to manipulate the underlying code. The community troubleshoots the code, but may also add new functions or snip bits of code for inclusion in other works. Open text projects are intentionally constructed to be built upon, re-encoded and redistributed. This kind of open text acknowledges the processes of meaning making and digital manipulation and incorporates them into the creative endeavor.

As any shopkeeper can tell you, windows not only display items but invite shoppers to gaze at them through their own reflection, literally seeing themselves in the product. Windows are always 'open' in the sense that viewers can look *at* them, peer *through* them and read *into* them. The authors of *Remediation* (2000) draw our attention to the 'windowed' computer interface through which we increasingly interact with all types of media. Bolter and Grusin present the computer interface (and digitization in general) as the latest substantiation of a media process ongoing at least since the inception of perspective painting. All media incorporate, translate and reposition the media that come before them. While the chapters of this volume focus to varying degrees on remediation processes, the computer windows analogy is apt because not only can multiple windows be arranged on a viewer's consciousness (as on a computer screen), but both the author and the viewer share responsibility for the specific arrangement and degrees of transparency or reflectiveness of the windows. This constructive activity draws the reader into the production, creating a 'hyperreal' production that is both mirrored and windowed; readers both access and reflect upon the text.

Most readers will be familiar with the concept of hypertext. Computer hypertexts, those links we point and click, are portals for excursions in countless directions. On the Web, hypertext allows surfers to jump from place to place, from idea to idea. Hypertext users are encouraged to shift their reading to various spots on a page, to flip pages out of order or to leave the text entirely, wandering through cyberspace until they find their way back again (or not!). There is another meaning of hypertext that – although not always explicitly discussed in the chapters of this volume – is important to this discussion. Gerard Genette uses the term to denote a text that is to some extent filled with earlier renditions. Stam and Raengo (2005) have adapted Genette's terminology to the study of film adaptations. The hypertext, in Gennette's sense, operates in relation to the 'hypotext' or anterior production of the text. In traditional film adaptations, the hypotext may be a novel and the hypertext the film adapted from it. But as adaptations accrete, hypertexts are drained into a collective hypotext that new hypertexts will draw upon. Stam asserts that hypertexts may not acknowledge – or even be conscious of – preceding versions, yet they will be adopted into the family of images, phrases, allusions and commentary that comprise the collective hypotext. These two senses of hypertext – as a multidirectional link to other texts and as the latest expression of an ancestry of meaning – will serve us well as we explore the process of film adaptation.

Adapting Remediation

Bolter and Grusin use the term 'hyperreal' to foreground the combination of presentation techniques in understanding media processes. We think it should be highlighted especially in understanding the process of media adaptations. Remediation draws our attention to the technical, and more interestingly, to the interaction of psychological and technological aspects of media production. In hypertextual media, technology is meaning, or at least partial meaning. Pleasure and understanding occur in constructing 'windows on the world' as much as in peering through them. The oscillation between transparency and reflectiveness is the essence of remediation. Media attempt to erase themselves in the act of presentation, giving viewers unobstructed access to the fictional world represented in them. But media can never be fully erased. Our sense of how media manipulate and arrange ideas comes into stark relief when texts are adapted from one medium to another. Immediacy is fractured; hypermediacy asserts itself. Bolter and Grusin describe this phenomenon as the 'logic' of media:

> *If the logic of immediacy leads one either to erase or render automatic the act of representation, the logic of hypermediacy acknowledges multiple acts of representation and makes them visible. Where immediacy suggests a unified visual space, contemporary hypermediacy offers a heterogeneous space, in which representation is conceived of not as a window on the world, but rather as 'windowed' itself. (2000, p.34)*

As Bolter and Grusin indicate, much of the pleasure of remediation for viewers comes from the juxtaposition of transparency – or immediacy – and the intrusion of filmmaking technologies apparent in hypermediacy. This has been a trait of film nearly since its inception. Audiences experience the sense of looking at the film, its technical and aesthetic qualities, while simultaneously looking *through* the film as a portal into the lives and stories portrayed on the screen. Remediation heightens our sense of the art and craft of filmmaking while simultaneously opening new opportunities to become involved in the story. While viewers at the Grand Café witnessed what they knew could not be true – a locomotive steaming into a basement salon – the technical achievement of film was enough to draw them into its world. The impact of remediation came from the 'gap between what (viewers) knew to be true and what their eyes told them' (Bolter and Grusin 2000, p.155).

In our age of digital special effects this double logic of doubled pleasure is heightened by each technical innovation. The 'bullet time' point of view employed by the Wachowski brothers in *The Matrix* (1999) defies the logic even of the computer-generated world in which Neo is battling. Nevertheless, it succeeds because it approximates the corresponding notion in our imaginations. If we were fighting battles in a virtual world and if we had the capacity to watch bullets in flight (and react to them!) then it would look something like this. The technical choices in *The Matrix* succeed where they draw us deeper into the imaginary world, even when we 'know' we are witnessing digital special effects. Computer-generated effects can give plots and characters an aura of authenticity beyond what a squishy translation of the Book of Revelations or the enigmatic deadpan of Keanu Reeves might typically evoke. The life of *The Matrix* beyond the film is sustained by further remediations as the film is adapted to video releases, video games, Web sites, and the multitudinous digital artifacts of cyberspace. Each of these remediations eventually develops into a collective hypotext, upon which new adaptations – including the films *Reloaded* (2003) and *Revolutions* (2003), but also the 'behind-the-scenes DVD *Revisited* (2001) – can be layered.

While Bolter and Grusin acknowledge that remediation can occur without 'conscious interplay between media', adaptation theory has been marked by comparisons between texts. Rather than compare, the chapters in this volume explore how films are adapted from novels, television, comics, games and other sources as part of an industrial strategy that attempts to trade on the recognition of particular works and the respect derived from literature in general. Repurposing texts gives audiences a place to 'start shopping' and helps films stand out in a crowded marketplace. However, there is always some discrepancy between the imagined world constructed by readers and the remediated world of film.

Remediation and Reflexivity

In terms of adapting texts to film, what audiences 'know to be true' derives not only from the properties of nature, but from the text(s) upon which the adaptation is built. Bolter and Grusin's approach to remediation in film is largely technical; they are primarily interested in the way the double logic of remediation alters the perception of, in our case, filmic material. But we must also concern ourselves with the shifts in meaning as texts are molded to the creative impulses and artistic competencies of various adaptors. Here we might be able to distinguish and make use of the concept of reflexivity. It is tempting to see remediation as a kind of 'technical' reflexivity, particularly when we are grappling with the variety of textual and technical transformations described in some of the chapters of this book. But it is important to see how reflexivity and remediation complement and overlap each other to utilize their conceptual power.

Remediation is literally 'the representation of one *medium* in another' (Bolter and Grusin 2000, p.45). The concept is most useful when contemplating how media are (re)presented in each other, as when the television program *Cowboy Bebop* is remediated in film. We can ask: How does the text change when it migrates from the living room to the theatre (and back again in DVD form)? What happens to the story it expands from serial 30 minute episodes to a single 90 minute movie? Remediation gains power as a conceptual tool in examining digital media, particularly in the windowed world of computers. What happens to *Cowboy Bebop* when fans cut and paste characters into an online version of *The Sims*?

Filmmakers (and audiences) create shifts in meaning regardless of the processes of remediation, however, as when one film is adapted to another. Stam (2005) describes reflexivity as the 'process by which *texts* foreground their own production, authorship, textual procedures, intertextual influences or their reception' (p.12). The distinction makes a difference. If we locate the impulse of remediation in the process of presentation, reflexivity occurs in the process of conceptualization. At one end of the spectrum, any medium can be remediated 'without apparent irony or critique' as when a film is copied to DVD; at the other end, the medium announces itself, as in the case of a windowed computer interface, with various windows containing text, video, photographs or music (Bolter and Grusin 2000, p.45). However, the texts inside each window may be reflexively conceptualized and understood, or not. Reflexive texts 'subvert the assumption that art can be a transparent medium of communication, a window on the world, a mirror promenading down a highway' (Stam 2005, p.12).

Remediation may in fact be an attempt to preserve transparency, as part of the oscillation between immediacy and hypermediacy. Jørgen Christensen explores overlapping remediation and reflexivity through the adaptations of Charles Dickens' novels. The various adaptations range from the reflexive, as when Oliver is portrayed as a dog or a robot, to the sincere, as when we see Scrooge and his ghosts trudge a linear course through the chapters of *A Christmas Carol*. All of these remediations pursue particular adaptation strategies, but only some are consciously reflexive. Both remediation and reflexivity alter their sources. Dickens is remediated in film, cartoons, television drama, and interactive DVDs. Each iteration reminds us of the power and limitations of the prior medium. More reflexive adaptations reference the collective hypotext not only of *Great Expectations* or *Oliver Twist*, but of Dickensian London, the serial novel, the unquenchable thirst for retold stories, and the industrial logic of repurposing popular texts. Reflexivity requires audience participation; there is no subversion without the initial assumptions. Ultimately, remediation shapes information; reflexivity communicates.

The Book and the CD

Writing about media adaptations is, of course, a part of the process of hypermediacy. In the chapters that follow, we draw attention to how texts are adapted and re-adapted and thus this book is drawn into a galaxy of technology and meaning while simultaneously spinning out a small constellation of our own. The compact disk that accompanies this text is part of our effort to be explicit about our reconstructions. But we must also acknowledge its existence as a text that both recontextualizes the filmic material and remediates it. Although the practice of including a CD with a book of this nature is not yet common, the nature of contemporary publishing makes it the next best thing to true hypertext. We imagined it first as a teaching tool, wherein students assigned particular chapters of the book would be able to view brief corresponding snippets of the films, video games and other texts discussed. But we could just as easily imagine readers who view each video first, then read the chapters. Or view, then guess what the authors are trying to say. Or read chapters then view random video clips to form their own 'windowed' understanding and generate their own theorization of media practice. We might then imagine those readers passing that understanding on to others as part of their introduction to this book, and those subsequent readers negotiating new meanings from the multiple chapters, video clips, authorial and directorial perspectives, in the process of what Stam (2005) calls the 'palimpsestic multi-trace nature of art' (p.15). Whichever strategy readers pursue, they will notice a 💿 emblem in the text, indicating that there is a clip available corresponding to the subject at hand.

Each of the eight subsequent chapters in this book is intended to provide a different perspective on the practices of media adaptation. In keeping with our understanding of openness and hypermedia, each chapter stands on its own and the book can be read in any order. Steen Christiansen investigates how emotions are adapted when *The Hours* is remediated from novel to film. Taking a narratological approach, he focuses on how filmmaker Stephen Daldry employs cinematography and *mise en scene* to evoke mood. Ove Christensen discusses another kind of mood when he defends Lars von Trier's adaptation of *Medea*. Critics and audiences howled when the telefilm debuted on Danish television, but Christensen argues that the director's sense of transgressing imagery and digital techniques de-familiarizes, and therefore resuscitates, the classic play. Michael Skovmand examines four recent films based in Shakespeare and aimed at youth audiences. Traditionalist critics have demeaned the films as 'dumbed down'; Skovmand revisits this critique and evokes the specific practices of filmmaking to challenge it. Kyle Nicholas explores the globalization and transmogrification of the Japanese anime series *Cowboy Bebop*. He investigates various remediation strategies – both industrial and fan-based – to understand how the Internet functions to disrupt and redefine the adaptation process.

Gunhild Agger identifies domestic-universal combination strategy at work in the adaptation of *Babette's Feast*. She argues that this adaptive strategy associated with filmmakers seeking both local and global audiences can actually be located in the production and reception of Blixen's novels. Jørgen Riber Christensen explores the intertextual potential of Charles Dickens' novels, particularly the more esoteric adaptations into television programs such as *Family Guy*, *Futurama*, and *South Park*, and in Disney films. He asks how and why Dickens is so ubiquitous and recognizable even in such peculiar and unlikely forms. The Spike Jonze film *Adaptation* is the subject of Bent Sørensen's investigation of genre, character and representation in the adaptation process. He argues that *Adaptation* is a meta-film that remediates a novel, books on screenwriting, autobiography and the filmmaking process itself in a merciless parody. Finally, Torben Poulsen explores the overlapping dimensions of comics and videogames and discusses how shifts in remediation and adaptation strategies have consequences for comic readers, filmgoers and game players.

Our goal for *Open Windows* is to take a fresh look at a process that has been ongoing since the time of Méliès and the Lumière brothers. The multiperspective, multimedia approach of this volume is warranted as filmmakers and audiences grapple with digitization and globalization. As the very physicality of 'film' changes and audiences become involved in new ways, our understanding of 'adaptation' must necessarily evolve. This volume is our attempt to be responsive to the changes before us and to open a dialog on these emerging processes.

SOURCES

Bolter, J.D. and R. Grusin (2000) *ReMediation: Understanding New Media.* Cambridge: MIT Press.
Genette, G. (1982) *Palimpsestes: La Littérature au Second Degré.* Paris: Seuil.
Putnam, D. (2000) *Movies and Money.* New York: Vintage.
Stam, R. (2005) *Literature Through Film: Realism, Magic and the Art of Adaptation.* London: Blackwell.
Stam, R. and A. Raengo (2005) *Literature and Film: A Guide to Theory and Practice of Film Adaptation.* London: Blackwell.

MEDIA REFERENCED

Cameron, J. (dir.) (1997) *Titanic.* USA: Paramount.
Columbus, C. (dir.) (2001) *Harry Potter and the Sorcerer's Stone.* USA: Warner.
Columbus, C. (dir.) (2002) *Harry Potter and the Chamber of Secrets.* USA: Warner.
Cuaron, A. (dir.) (2004) *Harry Potter and the Prisoner of Azkaban.* USA: Warner.
Gibson, M. (dir.) (2004) *The Passion of the Christ.* USA: Fox.
Jackson, P. (dir.) (2001) *The Lord of the Rings: The Fellowship of the Ring.* USA: New Line.
Jackson, P. (dir.) (2002) *The Lord of the Rings: The Two Towers.* USA: New Line.
Jackson, P. (dir.) (2003) *The Lord of the Rings: The Return of the King.* USA: New Line.
Méliès, G. (dir.) (1902) *A Trip to the Moon.* France.
Wachowski, A. and L. Wachowski (dirs.) (1999) *The Matrix.* USA: Warner Studios.
Wachowski, A. and L. Wachowski (dirs.) (2001) *The Matrix Revisited.* USA: Warner Studios.
Wachowski, A. and L. Wachowski (dirs.) (2003a) *The Matrix Reloaded.* USA: Warner Studios.
Wachowski, A. and L. Wachowski (dirs.) (2003b) *The Matrix Revolutions.* USA: Warner Studios.

Dig that Cowboy
– Textual Networks in the Adaptation Process

Kyle Nicholas

> *'All readers are filmmakers, in a sense'.*
> – Anthony Minghella, Director

In recent years the advent of new media technologies has transformed our sense of adaptation and with it our sense of authorship and authenticity. Media consumers, or 'readers', have always been active to some extent, selecting, combining and re-contextualizing portions of their favorite texts. But multimedia networks have both deepened and extended these activities in important ways. Employing digital duplication and production tools, global communities of network users now create and exchange media artifacts of ambiguous provenance. Members of these networks inhabit 'the shifted mediascape produced by the Internet' that distributes production and desire (Burnett and Marshall 2003, p.75). Their activities are blurring the boundaries between author and audience, and transforming the nature of media adaptations.

Cowboy Bebop: The Movie (Columbia Tristar 2003), a genre-bending jazz-noir anime featuring intergalactic bounty hunters and 'space cowboys', is an example of this process. Originally titled in *Knockin' on Heaven's Door*, the film was adapted from a Japanese television show that ran in 1998-2000. *Cowboy Bebop*, developed into *CowBe* in online communities, is a stylish blend of traditional Japanese anime with the sensibilities of American Westerns and the foreboding themes of 1930s film noir, set to a moody, often innovative jazz score. Its classic anti-heroes, Spike Spiegel, Faye Valentine and Jet Black, scour the universe for outlaws, collecting bounties to keep their rust-bucket spaceship afloat. Although the film is not as tightly scripted as the series, it allows more time for long, existential passages between the intense firefights and escapes associated with futuristic bounty hunting. The galaxy in the near future turns out to look a lot like contemporary Tokyo or New York, with its deep shadows, clanging subways, and constantly dripping rain. When the crew heads out of the urban landscape they are as likely to end up chasing through a Moroccan market or listening to the advice of an American Indian medicine man as rocketing to the red planet of another solar system. Scenes are infused with a bluish light, rain drips from awnings, splashes under car tires, and soaks Spike's turned-up suit collar. Yoko Kanno's score is equally eclectic, evoking Charlie Parker, Charlie Musselwhite, Johnny Cash and U2. Music is a star in this film and Kanno's albums have been top sellers in Japan.

The film distinguishes itself from most animation with its distinctly adult themes and brooding pace. The hulking Jet tinkers with his mechanical arm while he worries about money and holding the crew together. Faye, decked in a yellow vinyl halter and hot-pants, is always looking for the big score, her independence outweighing any loyalty to the crew. Spike shuffles, smokes, and scatters sarcastic comments motivated by a lost love and a drifter's penchant for turning good luck into bad. With the addition of an asexual computer-geek teenager, Ed, and chip-implanted Welsh corgi, Ein, the crew forms a dysfunctional family whose orbits will never quite align. In the tradition of Japanese commercial culture, *Cowboy Bebop* draws on a global mélange of iconic cool. The film evokes Bruce Lee and Melvin Van Peebles, Spaghetti Westerns and the Delta Blues, skate punks and The Avengers.

Cultural Mobility as Industrial Strategy

The series – now seen in more than 100 countries in 13 languages on Cartoon Network – and the film employ typical Japanese cultural production techniques, grafting US cultural icons onto their own regional form, and then exporting the hybrid back to the West (Gallagher 2004). Anime developed in a Japanese television market that is 95 percent self-sufficient; Japan imports very little television programming. On the other hand, the unique properties of anime, including its traditional storylines, use of Western icons, and adaptability to dubbing, give it a low 'cultural discount', making it perfectly suited for export, and more importantly, for global web-based communities. Young Americans – and the urban hip in most Western cultures – are drawn to anime because it remains unpredictable, 'colorful, exciting, strange, and Japanese' (Horn 1999, p.13-31). Japan has a particularly twisted relationship with jazz music. Perhaps the largest jazz market in the world, Japanese artists and fans still consider homegrown jazz inferior to the American form. For many Japanese, authentic jazz is the realm of black Americans and Japanese musicians, no matter how accomplished, can only be imitators (Atkins 2000). *Cowboy Bebop* offers different cultural hooks to Western and Asian audiences; each tries to read the other through the text and discovers something about the progression of their own culture in the process. This kind of semantic and cultural mobility is constitutive of Web communities based in pop culture.

In a strictly commercial sense, *Cowboy Bebop* is adapted from a television series that debuted on Tokyo Television with 12 episodes in the 1998 season. But fan activity has been an influential force in the construction and distribution of *CowBe* almost from the beginning. Although the first episode shown was hardly a hit, the series developed a small but loyal following throughout its initial run. When it was not renewed for a full season, those fans got active in chatrooms and online gatherings and made their feelings known to producers at Sunrise Entertainment. Always attentive to fans in cyberspace and sensing a potential hit, Sunrise produced another 12 episodes and sold the entire 24 episode season to WOWOW cable television. Before airing the episodes, Sunrise also contracted with its parent company Bandai, a Japanese toy giant and one of the largest producers of Japanese entertainment in the United States, to combine some episodes to laser disk for direct sale. Sales of the disks (generally collector's items for dedicated fans) were brisk, and helped generate an online buzz for the cable episodes. As the episodes arrived (with a new Episode 1 helping to explain the series to new viewers) online anime communities in Japan and around the world used the series to explore their own creativity and interact with characters and each other.

Communities of Content

Among other kinds of exchanges, fans create "shrines" dedicated to favorite characters, using digital tools and community dialogue. These are communities of content; that is fans of Bebop, as well as communities of creation, employing Flash software and XHTML editors to co-create textual extensions, as in this fan's shrine:

> *Welcome to Fatal Façade a shrine dedicated to Faye Valentine, the lovely bounty huntress in the awesome anime series, Cowboy Bebop. I realize it didn't take long for a new layout change but I didn't want to wait around either. I was beginning to become aggravated with the scroller and how everything on the site was*

too compressed looking... I finally added an Updates section so go see what's updated! If you have any questions or comments e-mail them to me otherwise feedback in the gbook is greatly appreciated! ... Now, go have some fun and explore in the wonderful world of Fantastic Faye-Faye!

Shrines such as Fatal Façade are not only dedications to characters, but practical applications of technical skills developed in front of our eyes. When Bandai began to release DVD sets of Cowboy Bebop, images ripped from the DVDs appeared almost immediately in the online networks. The images were manipulated into chat icons, gaming avatars, computer screen wallpaper, and a variety of other forms, all created alongside of, and competing with, 'official' versions licensed by Bebop's originators. This interplay between industrial media creation and fan – or user – appropriation and re-creation is now an integral part of the adaptation process. Minghella's 'readers' have always created movies in their imaginations. Now, they routinely create and distribute digital versions online in textual networks of activity and meaning.

Three Premises of New Media Adaptation

These evolving online activities have some implications for our understanding of media adaptations. First, we must recognize that all texts are potentially multimedia. This premise is hardly shocking to producers of Hollywood films or Tokyo television. Sunrise and Bandai, along with other partners, have not only adapted Bebop into a feature film, but have produced several *manga* (Japanese comic book) series, graphic novels, art books, anime guides and action figures, along with various DVD sets and four Bebop-inspired jazz albums by Yoko Kanno and the Seatbelts. Sunrise president Takayusi Yoshii characterizes this fluid enterprise as part of a 'borderless world of ideas', the result of corporate consolidation and diversification of media outlets: 'As new protocols are adopted, more and more people around the world are finding it possible to enjoy our creations; while at the same time we are able to form closer, real-time bonds with them as customers, and learn just exactly what they like – and what they want' (Yoshii 2002). These kinds of statements from corporate presidents continue the rhetoric of synergy, the grand idea of conglomeration in media industries that has had mixed results in the industry. But synergy has a different twist as non-commercial outsiders become partners in production and promotion. *CowBe* is the co-production of *Cowboy Bebop* (both the series and the film) and an imaginative and technically proficient online community. Commercial-industrial productions like *CowBe* now find themselves in dialogue with a range of fan-created artifacts. Digital tools and the global networks that support them have blurred the boundaries between production and consumption, and call into question claims of ownership of cultural products at any particular stage in their development. As these tools continue to mature and diffuse the role of an audience member will no longer be 'that of passive listener, consumer, receiver or target. Instead it will encompass any of the following: seeker; consultant; browser; respondent; interlocutor; or conversationalist' (McQuail 1997, p.129).

As fans alter *Cowboy Bebop*'s original storylines, Bandai responds with *Shooting Star*, a manga with familiar *Cowboy Bebop* characters in an alternative universe populated with new villains and heroes. In this sense, the series is twice adapted, first to a new medium, then to a new textual space, with an alternate back story and additional characters. In a traditional textual adaptation, this might seem a dubious proposition. Despite inevitable detail changes in any adaptation, the basic relationships and storyline must remain intact for the adaptation to remain credible. The textual properties of anime, *manga* and science fiction, however, lend themselves to myriad recombination. Producers can also count on a built-in fan base, as their commercial productions mimic user activities.

This kind of dialogic development of texts between originators and users indicates a second premise, that all texts are now networks of form and meaning. The notion of a preferred reading is problematized when dexterous users can quickly recombine and remediate the essence of any text. Industrially produced texts inhabit a universe in which they encounter themselves in endless variety of mirror worlds, shifted in both physical form and shared understanding. Plotlines, relationships, characterizations, and style – those very qualities that draw in fans – become infinitely malleable in digital networks. In this sense, the original Cowboy Bebop series is really just the DNA which, when combined with the emergent nature of online textual communities and the commercial exigencies of brand extension, is capable of producing all kinds of related creatures. Garvey describes this process as 'gleaning', wherein 'authors of texts leave surplus of meaning, sometimes obvious as ambiguity, which readers maneuver within, or scoop up, glean and reuse' (Garvey 2003, p.208). Fans have always gathered around popular culture texts as a way of forming community and extending the meaning of the principle text. Garvey describes 19th century scrap book makers gathering in farm houses to collect their favorite readings, newspaper clippings, photographs and other artifacts together into bound volumes. Scrap book makers cut, paste, rearrange and recirculate texts that are already meaningful to them, and in the process add meaning through the recontextualization of images and ideas. Reading groups, music appreciation societies, and other textual communities challenge and reinforce interpretations, distribute textual arcana and most importantly, form social relationships in and through texts. Janice Radway (1987) explored this territory in her analysis of women reading romance novels. In Radway's study, the women revealed an interest in more than escapist fantasy. Her women saw the novel as a way of securing private time and (mental and emotional) space, and as an essential connection to support mechanisms of other women. Henry Jenkins (1992) described how Star Trek fans create identity and community based on ideals initiated – or at least vocalized – by the fictional television series. Jenkins' 'fans' reveal themselves to be a heterogeneous group that re-purpose Star Trek in ways that fit into and reveal their deepest fears and highest aspirations for the society in which they play a part. As Jenkins notes (and the film *Galaxy Quest* hilariously parodies) Star Trek fans distinguish themselves through their obsessive pursuit of trivia and canonical recollections of episodes.

Most *CowBe* participants seem to forsake the rabbinical pursuits of textual analysis for more hedonistic rituals, constructing digital shrines to favorite characters. Whereas gleaners collect leftover meaning and *Trekkies* bond by reading into textual arcana, *CowBe* fans create media of their own and distribute it through networks that parallel and cross the commercial-industrial conduits. In the age of digital media and global telecommunications, fans have the opportunity to extend meaning and community in ways previously unimagined. Inexpensive digital creation and distribution are reducing the disparity in authenticity between original creators and those that contribute textual accretions.

Fans are at ease with a multiplicity of meaning portrayed in multiple media. Networks of meaning surround and penetrate *Cowboy Bebop*. Bolter and Grusin (2002) describe this emerging process of representation as 'remediation'. The process of remediation heightens the sense of authenticity by foregrounding adaptive processes, whether conceptual or technical. *Cowboy Bebop:The Movie* becomes *CowBe*, the community, though a shared appreciation of mediation processes and an understanding of the 'borderless world of ideas'. Whereas traditional film adaptations aim for immediacy, attempting to erase the process of re-presentation, *CowBe* inhabits 'hypermediacy', a more open construction that invites viewer dialogue:

> *The logic of hypermediacy acknowledges multiple acts of re-presentation and makes them visible. Where immediacy suggests a unified visual space, contemporary hypermediacy offers a heterogeneous space, in which representation is conceived of not as a window on the world, but rather as 'windowed' itself. (Bolter and Grusin 2002, p.34).*

In a digital era where all texts are multimedia and mutually constructed as networks of form and meaning, marketing and communal activity become inextricable. This third premise suggests that industrial marketing strategies are supplemented, contested, revamped and extended in textual communities. Users engage in several quasi-marketing activities, including (re)circulation, (re)interpretation, (re)distribution and (re)evaluation. At a primary level, all fan activity extends a media brand. *Cowboy Bebop* captures new potential audiences as its signs are transmitted through cyberspace, increasing the possibilities for web surfers to bump up against it. Web shrines, like *FayeValentine.net* keep fellow travelers up to date on developments in the online community, pointing to new digital products created both by industrial originators of Bebop and by its many co-creators in the online world.

Industrial/Communal Co-Production

Cowboy Bebop was created by a team experienced in anime and television work. Shinichiro and set designer Kawamouri Shouji created the look and feel of the series distinct from their previous work in popular series such as *Vision of Escaflowne* and *Macross Plus*. Shouji is referred to in anime circles as the 'King of All Mecha' for his fantastic weapon and spacecraft design (*mecha* refers to the particular aesthetics of machinery and other props prevalent in science fiction anime). Piano prodigy Yoko Kanno is a cult figure among anime fans for work on various series, including *Macross* and *Escaflowne*. Series writer Hajime Yatatae is credited with several popular anime series, including *Escalowne* and *Gundam*, but remains a mystery; several online anime guides speculate that the name is a pseudonym for an unnamed Sunrise staff member or group. Together the creative talent represents an anime 'superteam' that produced one of the most original television series of its era.

Sunrise and Bandai exploited *Cowboy Bebop* across the usual array of media outlets. The series was collected in several DVD sets, including a Deluxe Edition and the Perfect Sessions, which together have sold nearly one million copies. Sales of four soundtrack albums approached 100,000 before their release to the West. Tokyo Pop won the rights to produce two standard *manga* series, two graphic novels, and *Shooting Star*, an alternative telling of the *Cowboy Bebop* story. The television series was also adapted to a collection of art books and anime guides. These books present finished art work from the series and how-to-draw guidelines for illustrating characters and *mecha*. They represent an invitation to fans to recreate their favorite characters in *doujinshi*, or fan-created *manga*.

These are the traditional pathways of commercial exploitation and distribution of anime. Each represents a discrete window of exhibition, similar to traditional film exhibition windows. But in networks of form and meaning, exhibition windows become portals in another sense: fans have opportunities to engage the series as each new window opens and reflect back their aesthetic and cognitive interpretations.

Following its short television run, online fans have kept *CowBe* alive through online communities. Community members collect and distribute details about show creators and characters, trace the manifold pop culture references in Cowboy Bebop, and present 'spoilers' that contain episode synopses and insider information. These networks also spawn a great deal of 'fan-fic', or fictional stories written by fans. Fan-fic spurs new discussions, and in the digital age, transmutations of characters as they are reimagined, both figuratively and physically. LadyRazorsharp writes fan-fic that reads into the sullen Spike and the cunning Faye a budding romance based in a developing tenderness toward each other. In her stories, the two characters, who are constantly fighting in the series, overcome much of their defensiveness and reveal their 'true' attraction:

> *Faye glared daggers at her green-haired adversary. The more she looked at him, though, she noticed there was something unsettling about Spike's eyes. Was it the color, the brown that tended toward red, like garnets? Was it their shape, a flattened almond with a slight slant at the corners, hinting at Asian ancestors? Before she could decide, Spike let out a growl of frustration.*
>
> *'Let's continue this discussion somewhere a little more private, shall we?'*
>
> *He clamped a hand on the back of her neck, pushing her ahead of him down the corridor.*

Fan fiction is collected, critiqued and rated on numerous websites, such as FanFiction.net. As she expresses herself and shares her art in such online forums, LadyRazorsharp draws new female fans to the series.

Jupe, another female user, has created a romantic music video combining images ripped from DVD's with the MP3 of pop star Jewell, again extending *Cowboy Bebop*'s brand and meaning while earning credibility in the *CowBe* community and her own online fans. Jupe's blog is part of a network of relationships that blends online and off-line, public and private, commercial and non-commercial, all available to participants who link to her many pages through other sources. Media-savvy Jupe has included a variety of small character icons, or *gumi*, and text links so that other members of the *CowBe* community can easily link to her work. In a running dialogue about the film with all who enter her space, she is essentially marketing herself – both as a community member and as a technically proficient designer – to the larger world, but she does this in a way that connects and evokes participation, both in her life and in the commercial strategy of *Cowboy Bebop*.

Countless *CowBe gumi*, populate online chat rooms and game spaces. Using Photoshop, Paint BBS and other programs available on the Net, some users have created *gumi* for use in popular online games, including *The Sims*. These fan activities not only extend the *Cowboy Bebop* brand, but forge a new communal-commercial relationship between two global media companies, Bandai and EA Entertainment. Crafting *gumi* based in *Cowboy Bebop* develops strong linkages between artists and the commercial properties they emulate. Users also exchange *oekaki*, or 'doodles', through 'paintchats', online chat rooms for illustrators where users critique and rate the drawings. Highly rated *oekaki* requires both the appearance of authenticity and a new interpretation of the base characters. Although many artists still sketch and scan, putting their drawings down on paper before scanning them into their computers as digital images, digital tools for originating *oekaki* are increasingly available at low or no cost. As *Cowboy Bebop oekaki* are circulated through paintchats and other networks, the meaning and form of *Cowboy Bebop* characters are recirculated and the *Bebop* brand is extended physically and conceptually. The same kinds of digital tools are used to create *doujinshi*, or fan-*manga*. Here we have entire storylines, in *manga* form, created and circulated through the Net.

All of these products – Jupe's video, Deluxe Editions, *manga*, *doujinshi*, and others – compete in the same cultural market channels. On a recent day, more than 30 screen-pages of *CowBe* related items were for sale on eBay, the global online market. These items ranged from cigarette cases to plush toys to formally-designed Japanese scrolls. Various versions of the digital products mentioned above are also available, sometimes at highly discounted prices. *CowBe* effluvia intermix in cyberspace with participant-created digital texts and official commercial texts, creating a primordial soup of *CowBe* iconography. Each item is at once derivative and extensive, acting as building blocks for further textual extensions. Besides extending the brand, these products act as markers in the 'real world' and identify participants outside of cyberspace. For this reason, what at first glance appear to be trivial streams for second-tier marketers can function to increase *CowBe* community cohesiveness and to introduce a textual community to those who have never seen the film. These products, whether industrial or fan-created, recontextualize *CowBe*, cinching ever tighter the bonds between commercial production and the productive consumption of Web communities.

In the new digital economy, relationships, rather than things, are the primary units of exchange (Dolan 2000). Network participants create a set of expectations for films like *Cowboy Bebop*, as well as a pre-built fan base for its release. Film adaptations are born into a world where 'no single media event seems to do its cultural work in isolation from other social and economic forces' (Bolter and Grusin 1999, p.15). Film adaptations are necessarily multimedia events, stars in a constellation of form and meaning that is constantly expanded in ways that are simultaneously communal and commercial. As textual readers – or viewers – expand their social and technical capabilities in the Web, discussions of adaptations will need to consider how the multiplicity in any text alters the very essence of 'adaptation'.

SOURCES
Atkins, E.T. (2000) 'Can Japanese Sing the Blues? "Japanese Jazz" and the Problem of Authenticity', in T.J. Craig (ed) *Japan Pop! Inside the World of Japanese Popular Culture*, pp.27-59. Armonk, NY: M.E. Sharpe.
Bolter, J.D. and R. Grusin (1999) *Remediation: Understanding New Media*. Cambridge: MIT Press.
Burnett, R. and D.P. Marshall (2003) *Web Theory: An Introduction*. London: Routledge.
Dolan, D.P. (2000) 'The Big Bumpy Shift: Digital Music via Mobile Internet', *First Monday*, December. URL (consulted May 2005): http://www.firstmonday.org/issues/issue5_12/dolan/index.html.
Gallagher, M. (2004) 'What's So Funny About the Iron Chef?' *Journal of Popular Film and Television*, 31(4): 176-184.
Garvey, E.G. (2003) 'Scissorizing and Scrapbooks: Nineteenth Century Reading, Remaking and Recirculating', in L. Gittleman and G.B. Pingree (eds) *New Media 1740-1915*, pp.207-228. Cambridge: MIT Press.
Horn, C.G. (1999) 'Anime', in A. Roman (ed) Japan Edge: *An Insider's Guide to Japanese Pop Subculture*, pp.13-31. San Francisco: Cadence Books.
Jenkins, H. (1992) *Textual Poachers: Television Fans & Participatory Culture*. London: Routledge.
McQuail, D. (1997) *Audience Analysis*. London: Sage.
Radway, J. (1987). *Reading the Romance: Women, Patriarchy and Popular Culture*. Chapel Hill, NC: University of North Carolina Press.
Watanabe, S. (dir.) (2003) *Cowboy Bebop: The Movie*. USA: Columbia Tristar.
Yoshii, T. (2005) President's Greeting. URL (Consulted May 2005): http://www.sunrise-inc.co.jp/international/company/index.html.

Remediation Made Fun
– Examining the Dynamics of Comic and Computer Game Tie-ins

Torben Poulsen

The aim of this chapter is to expand our current understanding of media adaptations and extend the discussion of adaptations to twin passions of mine, namely comics and video games. Comics and video games have recently been adapted into a variety of media forms, including films, the topic of the present volume. This chapter is intended to introduce some of the theoretical exploration surrounding video games into the adaptation literature and to help develop a theoretical toolbox which can be readily used when approaching the adaptation interplay between comics, games and film. In this chapter I propose a method of tackling this issue of multimedia adaptation, in part relying on the theoretical construct of 'remediation' developed by Bolter and Grusin (2000). Given the very different nature of the media under study here, it is necessary to address the common denominators between them as well as point out what kind of adaptive problems are at stake when moving from one medium to another. The concept of remediation presents us with an analytical tool which helps explain the inner workings of every imaginable type of media transformation and narration. The concept will in short reveal how the various media recycle more or less recognisable traits from each other. Remediation is a term bound to the media *form* and not to the content as such – therefore the focus here will be primarily on which formal properties the three media share, bearing in mind that at times form also influences the content and that formal aspects can be seen on many levels (as the clips hopefully will clarify).

In keeping with the theme of the volume, the second aim of this chapter is to broaden our understanding of the term 'adaptation'. This project of expansion can be seen in the work of the other contributors to this volume, even where authors dealing with adaptive strategies do so specifically within the boundaries of two media formats, such as between text and film. It has to be stressed that even though it is very common to see works of literature translated to film or, more rarely, films translated to tie-in novels, other media transformations occur more often than one should think. When examining the vast jungle of popular culture it becomes clear that many of the films encountered, computer games played, and the comics read are interdependent. So this field of adaptation presents fertile new ground for serious academic research. In short both *'to boldly go where no man has gone before'* (Solow and Justman 1996 pp.143-149) and last, but not least, to have an excellent excuse for playing games, seeing films, and reading comics all in the 'interest of science'.

Simultaneously, this article proposes to demonstrate formal properties from the media forms by using nine clips from various media. The clips will hopefully clarify how various media traits can be translated and analysed, especially in relation to the adaptive stance. Aside from the formal properties, this chapter discusses some of the narrative similarities between the media formats. Lastly, it must be stressed that the chapter primarily will be concerned with the translation of comics and videogames into film, and not so much vice versa.

I will attempt to show how translating and adapting characters and narrative structures from the chosen media fields can be problematic in many respects and the following will primarily deal with two aspects:

- The potential hurdles filmmakers may face when adapting comic books and computer games into film;

and secondly,

- To show some of the solutions filmmakers have come up with to diminish the gap between the individual media formats.

The theoretical connections developed here focus on the formal properties of media as developed principally by Bordwell (1985), Smith (1995), and Shaviro (1997) in order to get closer to the inner workings of cinematic narration and representation. Bordwell, whose theorization is based in Russian formalism, shares a concern for media form with Bolter and Grusin. Smith and Shaviro both discuss the representation of characters in film and our relationship with them. I will connect these concerns with the videogame theory developed elsewhere, particularly in Poole (2000), Atkins (2003), and in King and Kryzwinska (2002) and the emerging comic book theory explicated in McCloud (1994, 2000) and Eisner (1986) in order to get an overview of how these media types are treated and perceived. Poole gives a general presentation of the evolution of the video game, whereas Atkins provides examples of video game analysis. King and Krzywinska discuss the possible theoretical interplay and overlaps between film formalism and game format and theory.

The analysed examples could have been identical to the ones many academic texts previously have touched upon. To give examples, when speaking of comics (or graphic novels) it is very popular to refer to comics such as Art Spiegelmann's holocaust fable *MAUS* or Allan Moore's reworking of superhero mythology in *Watchmen* and other works and link these texts to e.g. holocaust movies or theories of postmodernism. However, being an avid fan (and consumer) of popular culture, I have chosen to draw my comic book examples primarily from superhero comics, more specifically *X-Men*, *HULK* and Alan Moore's Victorian rewriting of popular culture *The League of Extraordinary Gentlemen* (henceforth LXG) in which protagonists known from Victorian novels are used in a new framework. Since the formal problems that arise when speaking of adaptation, or in this case remediation, are as relevant when using such examples instead of adaptations such as *Ghost World* or *From Hell*, which seem to have been made to appeal to a more limited audience. *From Hell* is yet another rendition of the Jack the Ripper story, based on several books on the subject, and *Ghost World* deals with the everyday life of the teenage girl, Enid.

In the same vein the video games chosen for exemplification are not the archetypes discussed so eagerly elsewhere such as *Myst* or *Black & White* (Poole 2000; King and Kryzwinska 2002). The *Myst* series relies heavily on stunning graphics and puzzles to create a unique game environment, and *Black & White* was one of the first so called 'God Games', where the player controlling 'the hand of God' as interface, had to regulate life on an island. Instead the paper will be discussing action/puzzle games such as the *Tomb Raider* and *Resident Evil* series. These games are primarily action oriented and besides solving a few puzzles (getting hold of passwords to operate a console or getting hold of keys to open doors) the aims of the games are primarily goal oriented with a strong emphasis on action and violence

– which makes them more difficult to adapt to film – and this struggle is reflected in many of their cinematic adaptations.

Lastly, it must be mentioned that the article will refrain from discussing various technical issues (possible poor acting in both games and film, badly made special effects, bugs in the game code, poor scripting, etc.) relating to the production of the media artefacts themselves. Although, it can certainly be argued that features like unoriginal dialogue or "hamming" could be an issue when writing about these types of adaptations (King and Kryzwinska 2002).

Remediation in Comics and Video Games

What then are the problems when adapting comic books and games to film? Media address their audiences differently, and this draws our attention to a cognitive problem with two major aspects. The first is the social aspect connected to the various media. Film is more often shared by an audience, either in a theatre or at home with a few friends, whereas reading comics and playing games are more often solitary pursuits (with the exception of multiplayer games). There is some common ground in the reception of both games and comics, in that it is possible to talk to other readers and players about the games or comics in question – but the reception of the individual artefacts is generally different and dependent on aesthetic judgements.

Secondly, it is important to centralize in our discussion differences in form. Even though film shares the characteristics with both games and comics – being primarily visual in nature – comics differ in being a series of still images combined with text. Comics also lack sound, which both film and games have (see Figure 1). Such observations may seem trivial but they reveal something about the incompatibility of the media in question.

Bolter and Grusin's (2000) term 'remediation' traces the act of appropriation in media from (at least) the development of perspective painting during the Renaissance. Their use of this term draws in part on ideas articulated by Marshall McLuhan, who claimed that various media were dependent on previous forms of communication: '[T]he "content" of any medium is always another medium. The content of writing is speech, just as the written word is the content of print and print is the content of the telegraph' 1964, p.8).

In *Remediation*, the authors pinpoint common denominators and relationships between the various expressions of media in our current media landscape. The authors' aim is to get their readers to think about how various media forms have influenced each other, and emphasize that new media types have always been recycling formal traits which can be found in previous media.

Bolter and Grusin define media as:

> [T]hat which remediates. It is that which appropriates the techniques, forms and social significance of other media and attempts to rival or refashion them in the name of the real. A medium in our culture can never work in isolation, because it must enter into relationships of respect and rivalry with other media. (2000, p.65)

They also claim:

> We cannot even recognize the representational power of a medium except with reference to other media. If someone were to invent a new device for visual representation, its investors, users and economic backers would inevitably try to position this device over against film, television and various digital graphics. They would inevitably claim that it was better in some way at achieving the real or the authentic, and their claim would involve a redefinition of the real or the authentic. (2000, p.65)

The concept of remediation could be compared to the notion of intertextuality, but whereas intertextuality is usually connected to narratives, to more or less visible relations and connections between individual texts, and even used to highlight the artificial nature of the textual construct in question, remediation refers to the interplay between media forms and not necessarily the messages the narratives try to convey.

One of Bolter and Grusin's basic claims is that the media, in whatever form they may take, uses two distinct styles or strategies of presentation. Beginning with perspective painting, media privilege the notion of immediacy, an attempt at making the medium transparent and encouraging the viewer to lose herself in the reality of the presentation. But, they argue, that media now achieve the effect through hypermediacy, where the medium in question not only recycles form and content, as per McLuhan, but 'windows' the content, so that the media references, particularly the formal aspects, are part of the presentation, e.g. part of what 'draws in' the viewer and renders the presentation 'realistic'. In short, the premise of remediation is that no media forms have evolved independently; they cannot effectively hide either their predecessors (the Web is obviously indebted to print and television) or the fact of their mediation. Remediation is the way one medium, as Paul Ward observes, 'appropriates the representational strategies of another, ostensibly in order to further its transparency/immediacy but with the apparently contradictory consequence of foregrounding the process of mediation itself' (King and Krzywinska 2002, p.128).

If a spectator accepts the gigantic dinosaur in *Jurassic Park* or Gollum in *Lord of the Rings* as being real, the media have succeeded in creating immediacy. We accept the creatures as being part of the story and can even feel threatened by or form empathic relations with the beings. But simultaneously, the effects which uphold this illusion in the framework of the film point directly to the fact that the creatures have been generated by a computer, and this is part of the reception (and enjoyment) of the presentation. In other words, immediacy is at work, but no matter how believable the effect, hypermediacy also renders medium itself apparent. This is often exemplified by the many 'behind-the-scenes' documentaries found on DVDs and in the media landscape. When we know how the effects are being made, we may interpret them differently.

Hypermediacy is where the connection and explicit links between the media forms become visible. How the comic book, computer game and film industries influence each other (or are 'present' in each other) is a complex matter. For instance, filmmakers have ventured into the field of comics – e.g. Alexandro Jodorowski, and comic book artists, such as Frank Miller, Todd McFarlane, Mike Mignola, Moebius (Jean Giraud) or Enki Bilal, have worked on films.

Although it is difficult to effectively diagram all myriad ways in which film, comic books and video games remediate each other in adaptations, it is possible to pinpoint some of the broader traits which the media share.

All three media are visual in nature, thus making 'visual representation' central to the model. Video games and film also share the element of 'sound' (i.e. music, speech and sound effects). They also share '3D environments'; although one cannot move freely about in the cinematic environment, the illusion of space is central to the filmic experience (Grodal 1999; Bordwell

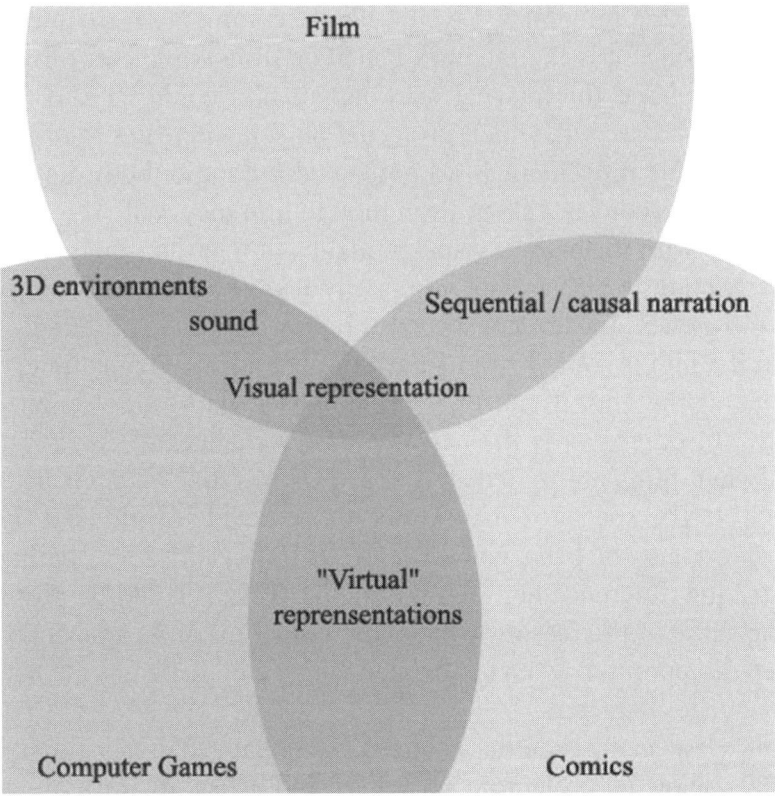

Fig. 1 – Overlaps between media.

1985, 1997). Comics and film, on the other hand, share the 'sequential or causal' narrative relations. That is to say that both comics and film by and large adhere to the Aristotelian notion of narration, with a beginning, middle and end.

The term sequential or causal narration is opposed to the interactive elements of games, where as I shall return to, which offer many different narrative paths to traverse. Comics and film are much more linear in nature (Aarseth 1997). By virtual representations I refer to the fact that neither the comic, however realistically drawn, nor the game – even though the game may use cinematic scenes or voices of actors – have the same similarities to our known reality as does film, i.e., we are able to relate to 'real' physical bodies and faces when seeing films, instead of artistic renditions of the same. Film has by far the highest visual modality of the three media investigated here.

Before turning to comics, I would like to comment on the medium of fiction film, since it is the medium I shall be discussing least formally. At its most simplified the internal workings of film could be said to be 24 frames of film a second, which projected on screen creates the illusion of movement. This movement is accompanied by audio, both diegetic and non-diegetic, to convey a story. Even though film may well present itself as the medium with the highest visual modality, film has, on a narrative level, some restrictions which are not necessarily at work when examining comic books and games. The level of spectator interaction is very limited.

Even if a film is complex in its narration, and leaves many unanswered questions at the end, it can only present itself with one version of the narrative. In other words the narrative never changes when re-watching a film (when films are remediated as DVDs multiple versions become a possibility). The spectator may notice more details overlooked the first time around, but the basic plot structure is static, and this is perhaps the most striking difference between the media. This, it could be postulated, is perhaps one of the reasons why comic book fans and game enthusiasts are often disappointed when confronted with a cinematic representation of their favourite characters.

Comics, especially superhero comics, have changed drastically since the late 1980s, allowing a plethora of writers and artists to work on specific characters. The comic book fan can chose from a variety of stories featuring his favourite characters (i.e. the origin myths of Batman or Spiderman may vary from artist to artist), and the comic book readers often have no problem in accepting this. This is just the freedom of comic book writers; an imaginary playground. However, when this character is suddenly portrayed by an actor, say Eric Bana in Ang Lee's *Hulk*, the protagonist is no longer a combination, or gestalt, of the various comic book renditions of him, but reduced to a singular form, and this singular form may not correspond with the one created by the readers of the various comics.

The same thing goes for computer games but here it is primarily on the level of narration. Many games have, as authors such as Stephen Poole (2000) and Barry Atkins (2003) argue, an extremely linear structure, though they want convey an impression of an almost gigantic internal world where many possibilities are available. A few (Japanese) games even offer several narrative paths to follow (e.g. Konami's *Metal Gear Solid*, *Silent Hill* or Square Soft's *Final Fantasy* series, etc), but can this interaction and multiple narrative structures be adapted to fit a film format? This is a question I will be returning to below.

The (Academic) Perception of Comics

For the most part, scholars paid little attention to comics for most of the 20th century. The odd exception might be the condemnation of comics due to their devastating effects on children, such as in Fredric Wertham's (1996) *Seduction of the Innocent* which in turn led to the establishment of the so-called 'comics code' in America (McCloud 2000, p.86). A possible explanation for this could be due to the fact that the academic communities and the public in general, have regarded comics as having little value apart from being light entertainment produced for children, usually located as counterweight to serious journalism in print news media. But since the 1980s interest has grown and various titles have begun to appear on the subject of comics. This interest in comics was presumably initiated when the comic developed into forms which were aimed at a more mature audience. Beginning in the 1960s underground comics have tried to appeal to an adult audience, and artists such as Robert Crumb or Gilbert Shelton captivated a generation of hippies with their weird and surreal renditions of life. But the newfound academic and analytical potential of comics was presumably inspired by Frank Miller's reinvention of Batman in the *Dark Knight Returns* (1986), Alan Moore's deconstruction of the superhero genre in *Watchmen* (1986), Eastman & Laird's self-published and hugely successful *Teenage Mutant Ninja Turtles* (1984), and graphic novels like Art Siegelman's semi-autobiographic (and Pulitzer prize-winning) holocaust fable *Maus* (1986).

The approaches to comics have often fallen into two distinct categories: one which uses film analysis to describe comics, ignoring the fact that sequential art forms preceded film by many years (McCloud 1994); and the other stressing the sociological importance or danger of comics. Neither of these is very helpful in understanding the true nature of comics. In order to make the same quantum leaps for comics as the school of cognitive sciences have done for film analysis it would be beneficial to turn to comic artists writing about their trade – Will Eisner and Scott McCloud.

Scott McCloud's 'Invisible Art'

Scott McCloud agrees with Will Eisner that comics are in fact 'sequential art' but in the introduction to *Understanding Comics* he questions Eisner's term, and instead defines comics as: 'juxtaposed pictorial and other images in deliberate sequence' (1994, p.9). McCloud claims that the major dynamic factor of comics is that the action is created in the gaps between the individual frames, or 'the gutter' as it is known in comic book terminology. These gaps share many similarities to the textual gaps in literature which theorists such as Wolfgang Iser (Lodge 1988) and Umberto Eco (1984) speak of. The major difference between these gaps is that, when reading an ordinary novel, the reader must use his mental apparatus to visualize the various items, surroundings, and characters which the text presents. In short, the reader must translate the text into images, but in comics the gaps which may arise when reading can possibly be filled out by the images shown alongside the text. The gaps in comics are of a visual/narrative nature, where the reader's imagination lies in making connections between one image and the next.

For instance, Scott McCloud explains this perfectly in *Understanding Comics*, where he demonstrates how two images prompt the reader to fill in the missing action him/herself. One image shows a man wielding an axe screaming "Now you DIE!" whilst another man in the foreground is running away pleading "no, no, no". The next image shows rooftops in darkness with the text "EEYAAA!!" superimposed on it. Scott McCloud argues;

> *The closure in electronic media is continuous, largely involuntary and virtually imperceptible. But closure in comics is far from continuous and anything but involuntary. [...] Every act committed to paper by the comics artist is aided and abetted by a silent accomplice. An equal partner in crime known as the reader. I may have drawn an axe being raised in this example, but I'm not the one who let it drop or decided how hard the blow or who screamed, or why. That, dear reader, was your special crime, each of you committing it in your own style. (p.68)*

By 'closure' McCloud refers to the mental process that closes the gaps inherent in the text itself. Film presents itself not as a series of individual frames, but as many film theorists suggest, we are quickly attuned to the rules of narration posed by cinema, and the brain fills in the gaps, creating the perception of a continuous, moving picture. Comics require something analogous to this 'filling in' process, except it is the narrative, rather than the form, that needs completing. Readers construct the action in their minds, rather than having every detail explained or illustrated. This is why McCloud terms comics an 'invisible art' – he claims that even people who are not avid readers can easily understand comics and this is why many manuals and internet sites use *'juxtaposed pictorial and other images in deliberate sequence'* to make their point as clearly as possible (1993, p.9).

A given comic book story can be told in almost unlimited ways by contrasting or harmonizing images, text, and so forth, the reading process of comics may not be as linear as many may think. McCloud argues that spectators not only read not from left to right, top to bottom, but moreover the readers' gaze, unlike with books or film, often strays around the page. So comics are not necessarily perceived in a linear fashion as film, nor do they adhere to the same structural workings as cinema.

Lights, Camera Action-comics!

Superhero comics seem important in relation to the discussion of remediation, because it seems that they are the ones most often translated into film. Even though films based on less action-oriented comics, (e.g. Sam Mendes' *The Road to Perdition*, Hughes Brothers' *From Hell* or Kinka Usher's *Mystery Men*) are being made, the action-oriented comic is perhaps the format that appeals most to comic book fans and action film fans alike, creating a wider market and larger profit potential. So monetary reasons could be the reason why it is often the Batmen, Spidermen and X-men that are translated into film more often than the more lyrical, weird or downbeat comics.

The superhero comic characters seem to draw their origins from various types of mythology – both Western and Eastern. Following in the vein of Joseph Campbell's book *The Hero with a Thousand Faces*, it could be said that many of these heroes are archetypes, in the sense that even though they may have superpowers each has an Achilles' heel. Furthermore, these heroes are often defined through their actions, and not as much through their intellect, as some of the clips on the CD aim to show.

In a fight scene taken from Bryan Singer's *X-Men* (2000) the villains and heroes are defined not only by their spectacular external characteristics

– more than their inner life – but moreover by their actions, their special abilities. 🎬 The clip shows both the aptly-named villain Toad and Cyclops use their respective powers. The second clip is also an action sequence, this time taken from Stephen Norrington's adaptation of Alan Moore's *LXG* (2003) which was subject to much criticism especially from the press who thought that some of the action sequences were too messy and left the spectator wondering who was fighting whom. 🎬

But as can be seen, when leafing through almost every recent superhero action comic book – (e.g. *Uncanny X-Men*, *The Authority*, or similar works), readers are constantly presented with fight scenes where the visual and spatial gaps must be filled at an alarming pace, and demands a vivid spatial imagination in order to realize who is fighting who and where. Often fights can take up whole issues of comics, with a plethora of characters fighting each other for some reason or the other. Therefore, it could be postulated that inexperienced comic book readers may find such frantic scenes of mayhem very confusing or even dull to read, but as is the case with other texts, the more you read, the more experienced you become at deciphering the meaning. To the experienced reader, such fight scenes are often appreciated because it is a culmination of events as well as it is in these scenes where many artists excel in their drawings. This is why the scene from *LXG* does not pose any problems for an audience who is familiar with comics (or indeed MTV and the 'new wave' of action cinema). In fact I would go so far as to claim that the action sequence is tailor-made for an audience which is used to these abrupt cuts from one spatio-temporal location to another.

Furthermore, from a cinematic perspective, 🎬 *LXG* is made in a tradition not usually seen in Hollywood action films. For instance, the camera and edits create a coherent spatial representation of the locale and relate the characters to each other in space. But moreover, as seen in many Asian martial arts and action films, the camera is positioned to accommodate impressive shots, rather than to follow the logical progression of the fight sequence (Bordwell 2000). In other words, the action not the story dictates where the camera is placed and which angles are used.

Video Games

Contrary to most comic book adaptations, many of the video game/film adaptations do not follow the narrative structures of the original, one of the reasons that visual representation is so important to this section. This is probably due to the fact that the films must not only appeal to the gamers but to a wider audience. More importantly when examining many computer games, the vast majority of narratives found here only work in relation to the interactive environment of the game. Video games can be played on an independent console or on a computer, but the salient point in this discussion is the notion of player control in human-computer interaction. (In our discussion of computer game adaptations, the Clips 3-9 will help to visualize how various remediation strategies are employed.) When playing a game, bad dialogue or inane plot twists are secondary concerns, the ludic perspective is dominant. When making film these things must adhere to the conventions of cinema. Perhaps most importantly the filmmakers have to craft credible characters out of digital archetypes which may not be incredibly complex. Film and games share not only the properties of sound, motion, and visual representation but most importantly also the illusion of three-dimensional space, with the major difference in games that the player is able to interact within this space.

Interactivity and the 'Passivity' of the Film Spectator

Interactivity continues to be a difficult concept to pin down. One of the ongoing discussions relates to whether interactivity could only be interpreted as one of two (Jensen 1998; Smith 2000):

1. interactivity signifies that one is allowed to change the form or the content, or
2. Interactivity signifies that one is able to change both form and content

The first view is the broadest and suggests that the user, by way of navigating a given hypertext or game, is able to get the required information or find the key to unlock the door at the end of the level. The second perspective is more complex, and suggests that the navigated text or game changes in accordance to the way the user navigates – i.e., that the player does not necessarily have to find the key, but could choose to blow the door off its hinges using the bazooka otherwise used for disposing of monsters.

The latter view is slowly getting more and more popular, and many new games allow the player to converse with the game in a non-linear fashion offering several different endings, in accordance with the choices made in the process of gaming. Konami's *Metal Gear Solid 2* even seems to mock the gamer (or at least entice the gamer that he or she has not seen the entire game) by showing him/her what possible paths the gamer did not investigate upon completion. Similarly another PS2 game, *Shadow of A Memory* (Konami), shows the final scene of the game and rates the player's performance at the end of the game. A possible ending could lead the protagonist to be imprisoned for eternity and the player would be given an 'F-' for his/her performance. Furthermore, in many of these games the forks in the path of the game are not always visible to the viewer. In other words, the nodes that influence the narration are not known to the gamer. To reach the best possible result then, one has to either play the game again more carefully or consult a walkthrough or a strategy guide. Although one can find a few films or books that are 'interactive', (e.g. Steve Jackson's multiple-choice adventures, or Milorad Pavic's *Dictionary of the Khazars*), this narrative branching is predominately a characteristic of video games.

Even though many film theories of late argue that the spectator is participating actively in a dialogical relationship with the film, the spectator is even more active when playing a game (Bordwell 1985; Smith 1995; Grodal 1994, 2004). When seeing a film, the spectator has no control over the actions of the characters but can only watch and interpret the images and sounds sent his way. In a gaming situation the freedom of choice is usually larger. For example although even most point-and-shoot games such as *Unreal 2* or *Max Payne* may be reliant on violence and offer very limited narrative possibilities (e.g. 'Should I shoot this or that guy, and what weapon should I do it with?') the graphics often are so visually stunning that the player also may wander the landscape or simply enjoy how the creators have pulled off the illusion.

But in an action movie, unless on DVD or video format, it is impossible to slow down the pace or to stop the narrative completely or to see what would happen if the protagonists went into the building by way of the basement instead of the main entrance. So what characterizes many games is the illusion of infinite interactive possibilities, and most importantly a fascinating 3D setting, which the player can explore. Lastly games could also be characterized by solving certain problems in a playful manner.

Scholars are often prone to discuss the values of a game as dependent on the game's relation to reality, and, as is the case with scholarly discussions of comics, video game scholars use terminology derived from film studies

(King and Krzywinska 2002). It would be fair to agree that some film terminology is beneficial when investigating games on a formal level (e.g. edits, camera movement even though no cameras have been used), however, as to 'realism' I agree with Stephen Poole (2000):

> *The lesson is that even with whiz-bang math programming, a videogame in important ways remains defiantly unreal. Video games' somewhat paradoxical fate is the ever more accurate modelling of things that don't and could not exist; a car that grips the road like superglue, which bounces uncrumpled off roadside barriers; a massive spacecraft with the manoeuvrability of a bumblebee; a human being who can survive, bones intact, a three-hundred feet fall into water. We don't want absolutely real situations in videogames. We can get that at home.(p.50)*

Furthermore, Poole's notion that it doesn't matter how far removed from reality the game is, as long as the game has a coherent internal structure, seems to be valid. It can be compared to the way science fiction and fantasy fans revel in the fictional universes which may defy logic, gravity and even common sense, but still have a coherent internal structure.

Games then, do not necessarily aim to be realistic, with the possible exception of simulation games (for instance *The Sims*). Games often represent a contrast to or break from reality, a form of escapism into a digital world where even the most serious threat remains within the confines of the fiction. In short, it could be postulated that many games exhibit narrative similarities to novels, films and comic books.

McCloud (1993) argues that it is important to establish a vocabulary in dealing with comics, it also would be beneficial for scholars to establish one for games. It is possible to encounter interpretation such as this one, which Poole (2000) uses to make a point:

> *We are looking at a neo-Marxist symbol of late capitalism. He is the pure consumer. With his obsessively gaping maw he clearly wants only one thing: to feel whole, at peace with himself. He perhaps surmises that if he eats enough – in other words buys enough industrially produced goods – he will attain this state of perfect selfhood, perfect roundness. (p.177)*

The game is of course Namco's *PAC-MAN* (1980). This example is meant to deliberately poke fun at (mis)interpretation, but it shows that the interpretative possibilities of games are virtually endless and often prone to fallacy if not being careful of what theoretical approach to utilise.

Translating Interactivity to Film

Possibly the most obvious difficulty filmmakers have when turning videogames into film is that film, as mentioned, does not share the interactive elements of the games. Furthermore, film cannot, in the same way as a game, allow the spectator to pause and enjoy the scenery. In other words the narrative cannot be affected by the spectator in film and the surroundings cannot be explored. However, some film adaptations of popular computer games try to accommodate this in various ways. Often the directors of these films choose to remediate recognizable traits which the player knows from the game, such as verbal expressions, rough plotlines, and, which is perhaps more often seen, it is the action trademarks from the games which are translated.

The film may include suggestive *special moves*, items or recognizable acrobatics known from the game directly in the films, such as Lara Croft's back-flips while drawing guns in the *Tomb Raider* film series 🌰, or the special power-moves in Paul W. S. Anderson's *Mortal Kombat* (1997). The tendency can also be reversed in the film tie-in's import or remediation of visual and auditory tactics lifted directly from the films. Examples include the recognisable theme music in EA Games' *James Bond* series, wall climbing acrobatics in Atari's game version of the *Matrix*, and bullet time in *Max Payne*.

At times some films even show the main protagonist being controlled by other parties, as the comparison 🌰 between the game *Tomb Raider Chronicles* and the first *Tomb Raider* film shows. In this case it must be the film which remediates the scene almost directly from the game, since the game was published in 2000 and the film adaptation was released in 2001.

If a scene shows a person in front of a computer, the player may draw parallels to his/her own gaming situation. Thus the game *hypermediates* the gaming situation itself – not only by explicitly pointing to the media form, but simultaneously the scene allows no control over the game avatar – in this case Lara Croft. This is a shift in the immersion of the game, the computer changes from being an interactive platform to a more traditional medium like film or television where the events are being transmitted in a one way system:

    Scene: (media) → (receiver)

    instead of

    Gaming situation: (media) ↔ (receiver)

The use of the laptop and the communication between Lara and friend seem identical. Angelina Jolie is, like the computer game character, identified by skimpy clothing and braided ponytail, but the communicative situation between the scene and the audience is different. The spectator can by no means control the cinematic Lara, and thus the film tries not only to remediate the gaming situation, but the insistence of showing surveillance camera monitors is remediating video, and thus the scene references not only on the digital medium of the game but on the 'reality' levels usually connected to the surveillance monitor. It could also be noted that the surveillance monitors could be seen as making the media transparent.

    The audience may, in the words of Murray Smith (1997), align their own personality to that of Lara or even Lara's helping hand, but they cannot intervene. It is also interesting to note that she is giving the instruction, '*You have to be my eyes*', instead of '*you have to guide me*' – and in this way the film tries to achieve the same feeling of hypermediacy as the game does.

Fleshing out Digital Characters

Many videogame-based characters have little or no background. What aspects of his youth made Super Mario choose the career of a plumber? Is Duke Nuke'em really a duke, if so where lies his estate? The characters of games, from a literary standpoint are extremely flat, perhaps deliberately so. Game players will have fewer problems in relating or aligning themselves with game avatars when characters are not too definitively drawn.

    Returning to Tomb Raider 💿 we can compare the opening scene of Jan DeBont's *Tomb Raider II – The Cradle of Life* (2003) and the second instalment of the Eidos Entertainment's game *Tomb Raider 2 – The Dagger of Xian*. Note in the clip how the director inserts visual cues that can be recognized by game players, such as the similar movements of characters in the game and the film. The scenes have been translated so directly as to cater to those in the audience who have played the games and know that such acrobatics define the Lara Croft character. If the spectator, in other words, finds that the film is regressing too much to fit standardized Hollywood narration, and perhaps grows slightly irritated with the fact that they are no longer in control of the action, these sequences will reaffirm that the character we are seeing is in fact Lara Croft, since these moves are so clearly identifiable as hers. Furthermore, it is striking that the opening scenes from both *Tomb Raider* films have such traits. In the first film, we see Lara combating a huge robot, and in doing so she is drawing both guns, firing while back-flipping – a trademark game-manoeuvre – once again as if to fulfil the game players' wants and needs as soon as possible.

Narrative Strategies in Videogame Adaptations

Narration in games is also very different from films. In games, and especially in the games mentioned in this article, the main character dies a thousand deaths before the narration ends and the gamer is rewarded with the final full-motion video scene, game score and other such accolades.

In Hong Kong cinema it is not uncommon that the pugilistic hero dies near the end of the film, but in the Western tradition of action cinema it almost unthinkable to have Bruce Willis or Arnold Schwarzenegger die in the end. That a character dies innumerable deaths in the course of a computer game poses no problem for the player – with regard to narration. Often it is simply a matter of restoring a previously saved game, and the player/avatar is back on track. When replaying a game, the game play is not only easier, due to the fact that the player knows the goals and dangers inherent in the game, but when recalling the narration the player, it could be argued, remembers the linear story of the game – and not the numerous times s/he has died during the game. This leads to the understanding of a game not as a fragmented narrative, but a perception of a dynamic (and in retrospect linear) storyline.

Many games employ scenes which primarily function as mood markers or as relaying vital information to the storyline, endowing the game with some basic narrative structure. Often such scenes also provide motivating factors for the player to continue. For example in Capcom's PS2 game *Resident Evil: Codename Veronica* (2000), the motivation in the scene could be 'what have caused all these dead people to suddenly want to eat my brains' – but more importantly the clip shows how a scene can be presented. 🎮 There are three shifts in modality in less than a minute; we move from player-controlled game play to a scene generated by the internal graphics engine (in programming terms known as an 'on the fly'), to full-motion video in a much higher visual quality, and then back to game play. The scene also shows how some games adapt cinematic styles – if not actual techniques – such as dynamic camera angles and rapid editing in order to heighten the suspense and the attention of the player.

The loss of control in the scene is very similar to those scenes in horror films where the protagonist is faced with mortal danger often represented by the monster or monsters. In such cases the protagonist, and the spectator aligned with the protagonist, is rendered helpless. The spectator is not able to help the protagonist, shout out or interact with the action presented to us. The frustration of not being able to interact in the game may lead to a feeling of horror and is even increased when the joypad 'rumbles' each time a zombie grabs the character – reinforcing the feeling that the player is still immersed in the game, yet unable to interact (It could be noted that the joypad also 'rumbles' during ordinary game play if the player/avatar is attacked). Also note the appearance of 'Widescreen' bars – which gives a visual cue to the player that the action is beyond his/her control.

Paul W. S. Anderson's adaptation of *Resident Evil* (2002) shares many of the narrative features and characters of the first two games by Konami. The scene from the film is entitled 'Obligatory BOSS Battle'. 🎮 Even though such final confrontations are often seen in horror/action films, the analogy is to the game. Most games have various powerful antagonists placed at key moments during game play, and these are usually more difficult to defeat than other monsters. The final battle in the case of the *Resident Evil* film is an almost direct translation of the final stages of the *Resident Evil 2* game, wherein gamers battle a very similar looking entity before a scene displays the dramatic escape of the protagonists by train. Once again, spectators with intimate knowledge of the game may recognize and appreciate this scene, whereas audiences who have no prior knowledge of the games may just perceive this monster as the 'obligatory' final confrontation between good and evil.

Notice the way the camera sways around Alice (Milla Jovovich) when she is crouching down, emulating the way in which spaces in computer games are often shown. It is also worthwhile to notice that computer graphics have been used both for the creation of the monster and the ultra slow moving bullet fired from Alice's gun. In short, the film both hypermediates computer graphics and uses them to create immediacy through believable effects.

Remediation in Overdrive

In some instances video games and film have become almost indistinguishable, as in Sakagushi and Sakakibara's animated film *Final Fantasy – The Spirits Within* (2001). This film can be perceived as a state-of-the-art computer-generated animation film, but it also appeals directly to an audience who has played the *Final Fantasy* games. The major appeal of his film may lie in the fact that it has the world's first full-length scene remediated in the form of a feature film. The relationship with the popular Japanese role-playing game series *Final Fantasy* is evident. Every game in the series creates a unique world, mixing science-fiction, steam punk, medieval settings, and fantasy elements with Japanese oddities. Common denominators between the games include the idea of the importance of spiritual energy and metaphysical questions about the soul and identity. Even though these themes are apparent in the film, their introduction questions the notion of reality, another form of hypermediation and intertextuality.

The scene opens with a lush rendition of an alien landscape and a realistic human figure placed within this landscape. We are so impressed with the animation, the texture of the skin and the high visual modality of the images that the images appear hyperreal, evoking Baudrillard's ideas of the artificial surpassing the real (1994). But this hypermediacy is further complicated when we realize that what we have initially taken as the reality within the confines of the fiction is but a dream – and even a dream which is stored in a futuristic computer. The 'save (yes/no)' which appear on the protagonists display also remediates the gaming situation, where (especially in games like the *Final Fantasy* series) it is imperative to save the game often, if wanting to complete it, and as such also works as a remediation/intertextual reference to the gaming situation itself. In this way the animators have not only commented on the medium itself but also one could speculate that the film is in fact merely the director's own recorded dream. The introductory sequence has, to my mind, the same narrative layers as in *The Matrix* (1999) with one major exception: in *Final Fantasy* everything, with the exception of the actors' voices, is created digitally, and thus the references to any known reality have been almost eradicated.

Video games are adapted to film, and film is often integrated directly into video game adaptations in order to simulate an immersion into the film itself. Even though it is not uncommon to mix film with computer graphics (e.g. videogames such as Origin's *Wing Commander* series have used digitized actors in virtual settings) the level of integration in EA Games' *Lord of the Rings – Return of the King* is quite stunning. 🎬 The game is an adaptation of the film, which in its own right is an adaptation of J.R.R Tolkien's books (1954-55). What is interesting is how players are introduced into the game. Though the game itself is a very banal fighting game, players are transported into the game universe by means of the film clip. As in *Resident Evil* 🎬 the visual modality changes when the game turns from filmed scenes to an interactive environment: the illusion of controlling the character is very effective indeed.

The game also expands both the film experience and the narration of Tolkien's novel. Upon completion, players may choose alternate characters to take on quests reserved for specific characters in the original story. (For instance, one could choose Gandalf to fight the giant spider, Shelob.) This violates the original narrative structure and exemplifies the type of interactivity where one can freely change both form and content of the game.

Peter Jackson's film (2003) has been integrated directly into the game giving the impression that the game is in fact emulating the 'interactive film', a term often used to market games. The game's back cover blurb states: '*Live the movie – be the hero!*' But is this really true? Even though the game has very stunning graphics, it is basically just another hack'n'slash game. The question is, do we really want an interactive film, and is it possible at all to create one? What does a high level of interactive choice do to the narrative structure, and is it possible to have games that are non-linear to such a degree that the freedom of choice of the gamer is virtually endless? If so, what would be the attraction and goals of such an imagined game? Lastly, how would this type of game be technically feasible from the perspective of game designers? Currently the closest thing to such narrative/interactive freedom lies in the multiplayer on-line role playing games (MORPG) like *Neverwinter Nights* and the like. In games like that it is possible for users to assume the role of Dungeon Master and create the basic structure of the game world – down to monster design and level design. Players can then interact in this world and make choices not necessarily dictated by a predetermined structure. However, there are still rules (physical boundaries, fixed scores, etc) which cannot be altered ad infinitum.

In *The Hulk* (2003), the cover art for the game is virtually identical to that of the film. Marketing copy on the game packaging states, '*Following the events of the blockbuster Universal Pictures film…*' Actor Eric Bana plays Bruce Banner in the film and lends his voice to the game, strengthening the relationship between film and game. But as can be seen from the clip, the game does not try to remediate images taken from the film. 💿 Instead the game uses graphics that seems to originate from the Marvel comic or a traditionally animated version of *The Hulk*. In this way the game remediates multiple media, seeming to present all of these media forms at once. Thus the clip illustrates the multiplicity of hypermediacy where a single format points to film, animation, comic book, and videogame simultaneously. The future may bring us a much closer convergence between individual media forms, to such a degree that it perhaps will be nearly impossible for future scholars and critics to distinguish between individual media forms, and to decide which medium is in fact remediating which.

Concluding Remarks

Bolter and Grusin's idea of remediation, although problematic in some instances, is both a flexible and powerful tool to explore adaptive strategies across various textual forms. Even though the boundaries between film, comics and games become increasingly blurred our understanding of remediation reinforces the need for close analysis of both form and content of the media product in order to distinguish the defining traits of each individual type. But as the chapter has shown, the remediation perspective also helps pinpoint where the various media types overlap. The three media types discussed in this chapter share similar formal traits (Figure 1), and this observation deserves more investigation and discussion.

Filmmakers are naturally very aware of the remediative processes of the media, and that by being aware it is in fact possible to successfully transpose an interactive medium into a linear format or the other way around. I hope to have demonstrated that it can be beneficial to investigate the forms and properties of the original medium in comic or video game adaptations as this is bound to influence the choices filmmakers and scriptwriters make. It would be beneficial to also look at computer game theory when analysing film adaptations of video games, for instance, or to look at theories on graphic art and comic books when dealing with cinematic adaptations of these works. The representational choices filmmakers, comic book artists or videogame programmers take often determine whether the adaptation seems to be true to the original format.

SOURCES

Aarseth, E.J. (1997) *Cybertext: Perspectives on Ergodic Literature*. Baltimore: Johns Hopkins University Press.
Atkins, B. (2003) *More than a Game: The Computer Game as Fictional Form*. Manchester: Manchester University Press.
Baudrillard, J. (1994) *Simulacra and Simulation*. Ann Arbor: University of Michigan Press.
Bolter, J.D. and R. Grusin (2000) *Remediation: Understanding New Media*. Cambridge: MIT Press.
Bordwell, D. (1985) *Narration in the Fiction Film*. Madison: University of Wisconsin Press.
Bordwell, D. (1997) *Film Art*, 4th ed. New York: McGraw-Hill.
Bordwell, D. (1997) *On the History of Film Style*. Cambridge: Harvard University Press.
Bordwell, D. (2000) *Planet Hong Kong: Popular Cinema and the Art of Entertainment*. Cambridge: Harvard University Press.
Campbell, J. (1993) *The Hero With a Thousand Faces*. London: Fontana.
Eco, U. (1984) *The Role of the Reader: Explorations in the Semiotics of Texts*. Bloomington: Indiana University Press.
Eisner, W. (1986) *Tegneserien & den Grafiske Fortælleteknik*. Denmark: Stavnsager.
Grodal, T.K. (2003) *Filmoplevelse*. Frederiksberg: Samfundslitteratur.
Grodal, T.K. (1999) *Moving Pictures: A New Theory of Film Genres, Feelings, and Cognition*. Oxford: Oxford University Press.
Jensen, J.F. (ed) (1998) *Multimedier, Hypermedier Inteaktive medier – Fisk Serien 3*. Aalborg: Aalborg Universitetsforlag.
Klock, G. (2002) *How to Read Superhero Comics and Why*. London: Continuum.
King, G. and T. Krzywinska (eds.) (2002) *Screen Play: Cinema/Videogames/Interfaces*. London: Wallflower Press.
Lodge, D. (ed.) (1988) *Modern Criticism and Theory: A Reader*. London: Longman.
Landlow, G.P. (1992) *Hypertext 2.0*. Baltimore: Johns Hopkins University Press.
McCloud, S. (1994) *Understanding Comics*. New York: Harper Collins.
McCloud, S. (2000) *Reinventing Comics: How Imagination and Technology Are Revolutionizing an Art Form*. New York: Harper Collins.
McLuhan, M. (1964) *Understanding Media: The Extensions of Man*. London: Routledge.
Pavic, M. (1989) *Dictionary of the Khazars*. London: Vintage.
Poole, S. (2000) *Trigger Happy: Videogames and the Entertainment Revolution*. New York: Arcade Publishing.
Shaviro, S. (1997) *The Cinematic Body (Theory Out of Bounds)*. Minneapolis: University of Minnesota Press.
Egenfeldt-Nielsen, S. and J.H. Smith (2000) *Den Digitale Leg*. Copenhagen: Hans Reitzels Forlag.
Smith, M. (1995) *Engaging Characters: Fiction, Emotion, and the Cinema*. Oxford: Oxford University Press.
Solow, H.F. and R.H. Justman (1996) *Inside Star Trek: The Real Story*. New York: Pocket Books.
Wertham, F. (1996) *Seduction of the Innocent*. Mattituck, NY: Amereon Ltd.

Adaptation in *Adaptation*
– A Real Fictitious Story(line)

Bent Sørensen

Adaptation (2002) (directed by Spike Jonze, screenplay by Charlie Kaufman) is a movie which addresses head-on the issues of adaptation, genre, character and representation. The movie is 'quite simply' a story about a screenwriter (this real fictitious character is also named Charlie Kaufman) who is given the impossible task of creating a Hollywood movie out of an intellectually restrained and cool piece of New York non-fiction (the book *The Orchid Thief*, written by Susan Orlean (real book, real writer)). Kaufman (the character) increasingly stumbles over problems with his research, with his personal life, and with the conditions his Hollywood employers impose on him. The end result is a monumental writer's block, which Kaufman can only exorcise by taking advice and inspiration from unlikely sources, such as his suddenly successful twin brother Donald, also a screen writer – although not real despite the fact that he has a fan website and was nominated for an Oscar – but of the most clichéd type of Hollywood genre drivel. Both brothers, real and fictitious, are played by Nicholas Cage in the movie. Other sources include Susan Orlean, with whom he develops an obsessive, masturbatory fascination; the main character of *The Orchid Thief*, John Laroche (who really was/is an orchid thief); Robert McKee, a real Hollywood screen writing guru (author of *Story: Substance, Structure, Style and The Principles of Screenwriting*, a real manual); and, chiefly, his own personal life (as he writes himself into the adaptation of Orlean's book).

The movie culminates in a number of genre twists, highlighting the problems of representation made particularly obvious by the adaptation process. This article makes three main claims: namely that *Adaptation* is a metafilm about adaptation as a co-creative process; that *Adaptation* is in fact an adaptation of both Orlean's and McKee's books, as well as a meta-adaptation of the conventions of autobiography and Hollywood's entire megatext of genre films; and finally that all these intertexts, including *The Orchid Thief* (a fact which has gone unnoticed by reviewers and critics, as well as by Susan Orlean herself), are mercilessly parodied in the process.

Adaptation as a Metafilm

Just as fiction has a self-reflexive mode which can be termed metafiction, the film medium has a self-reflexive mode which can be termed metafilm. This mode has been used with increasing frequency over the last 20 years, both in mainstream Hollywood movies and in independent and national filmmaking. Among the spectrum of features that signal the metadimension to film we shall focus on the following: ostentatious intertextuality; self-reflexive paratext; the use of filmmakers and other creative professionals as characters; the use of writing, filmmaking, screen writing etc. as themes in films. These features roughly correspond to the three mildest manifestations of metafictionality in Patricia Waugh's poetics of metafiction (Waugh 1984), only transposed to the film medium.

In fiction the mildest manifestations of meta-elements consist in plot, character and thematic features found in relatively traditional texts, such as the *Künstlerroman* (artist's novel) genre. These manifestations only function as meta-features when read as an allegory of general import or as carriers of (auto)biographical specificity. Thus the presence of artists in fictions may lead us to either think that the text is a disguised autobiography or at least a biographical text based on a real artist's experiences, or to think that the writer is using the figure of the artist to say something of general allegorical import about the position of the artist in a given social, historical situation. A story about a struggling artist who finally reaches commercial or artistic success at a certain price may well carry as its point a caution, either that society's norms should be transcended at all costs, or that society's norms will always crush the individual's dream of freedom (of expression). Similarly the overcoming of artistic obstacles invites a reading of this transcendence as a triumph on the personal level for the artist in question. Thus by writing something the writer accomplishes a change for the better in his/her real life, which invites the viewer to make a similar analogy to his/her own life. All these considerations can be applied equally well to the film genre we might term *Künstlerfilm*. *Adaptation* and indeed all the existing films based on Kaufman's screenplays (*Being John Malkovich*, *Human Nature*, *Confessions of a Dangerous Mind*, *Eternal Sunshine of the Spotless Mind*) can be seen as attempts at creating an ironic meta-*Künstlerfilm* subgenre.

All texts are accompanied by paratexts that frame them, open them and close them. These paratexts function on a macro-level of textual circulation to make texts readable, marketable, and consumable (Genette 1997b). Paratexts, such as titles, subtitles and other textual demarcations of divisions, credits, as well as other accompanying texts of a paratextual nature (in the film medium: DVD-covers, posters, trailers, promo-interviews and other commercial material) can be used to establish meta-effects. Part of the creation of the meta-dimension is done via the use of intertextual references to other texts which the model reader (or viewer of the film in question) is expected to be familiar with. We shall return to this particular area shortly. Other meta-functions of the paratext include self-reflexive titles (in film it is hard to find a better example of this than *Adaptation* itself), or subtitles that indicate genre (in film, for instance, 'the musical', 'thriller' etc.). DVD chapter titles can add a belated meta-dimension, since this information is not available to viewers of the movie in theatrical screenings (unless chapter titles are included in the film as captions or similar textual information). Posters and trailers, which function in the marketing of film in a similar manner as blurbs or promotional excerpts do in the book medium, can also add substantial meta-effects, for instance by blurring the identities of actors and characters. All of the above techniques are in full use in the case of *Adaptation*.

Intertextuality in the broadest sense of the word contributes to the construction of meta-dimensions in texts which, when we realize that they all relate overtly or implicitly to already existing texts, can then be seen to be based on palimpsests (Genette 1997a) on top of which they are written as 'new' texts. The notion that all texts are participating in a circuit of palimpsesting and intertextual connections between texts, is of course, on a meta-level, highly pertinent to this article, since these processes could all equally well be termed adaptation and/or remediation processes. In the case of adaptations, i.e. films based on previously written texts (novels etc.), this parallel is particularly pertinent. The potential number of pre-existing texts which are adapted through the remediation of a screenplay into a movie is thus nearly infinite. However, all films will have a number of manifestly present intertexts they explicitly refer to. These may be filmic texts, belonging to the *megatext* of a given genre of film, or they may be literary or other written texts. In the case of *Adaptation* the obvious intertexts are, of course, Orlean's *The Orchid Thief*, but on a slightly more subtle level also McKee's *Story*. The latent intertexts are the Hollywood genre-megatexts and the general textual conventions surrounding autobiography.

Adaptation as Metafilm in Terms of Plot, Characters, and Themes

Kaufman and Jonze's film uses the theme of writing in the allegorical fashion which was outlined in general terms above. For Charlie Kaufman, the character, (in future references this character will simply be named 'Charlie' in an attempt to distinguish him from the biographical, extra-diegetic person, 'Kaufman') the obstacle of having writer's block is equivalent to having a stagnant life. He is incapable of succeeding romantically and financially unless he overcomes the creative obstacle. This banal condition is instantly recognizable as a standard feature of texts about personal growth or *Bildung*. The stage is thus set for a story about a struggling artist who needs to exorcise personal demons to produce an important text with essential life lessons served up for the viewer.

The particular twist to Charlie's plight is that the creative effort he is required to do is what the film industry considers a secondary, technical form of creation, namely the adaptation of an already existing text. This apparently straightforward act of secondary creation turns out to be too much for him, since the condition for overcoming his block by necessity becomes a life investment for him. Thus, he must write himself into the script, contaminating Susan Orlean's 'clean' text with his own messy story. This violates the code of professionalism in Hollywood's simplistic reduction of adaptation to a craft, rather than an art. Kaufman's message is thus inherently satirical of the film industry's notion that any text can be adapted, by virtually any hack craftsman.

The theme of artistic production quickly turns out to be omnipresent in the film. Virtually every character in the script is a writer (Charlie, Susan Orlean), a wannabe writer (Donald Kaufman), a professional in the writing and/or film industry (McKee, and various editors such as Valerie), or someone who dreams of becoming an artist (Laroche, who actually is a born storyteller). The *Künstler*-environment is, therefore, overdetermined in the film. Over and above that, the creative process is described in great detail, from at least five different viewpoints: Susan Orlean's description of the genesis of her book; McKee's seminars and personal advice to Kaufman and any other potential screenwriter who is willing to pay to listen; Laroche's mythomaniacal constructions of his own life (as a collector and a preserver of cultural heritages); Donald Kaufman's bumbling efforts at plot construction out of the debris of genre clichés; and Charlie's mixture of all of the above strategies in the creation of his own mock-heroic autobiography.

The final rounding out of Charlie as a successful artist entails all of his literal or metaphorical collaborators paying a price and learning painful life lessons. Donald Kaufman, of course, pays the supreme price, since he gives up his own 'life' in the process of completing Charlie's script. Orlean is fictionally revealed as a drug and sex fiend and therefore personally contaminated in her previously pristine coolness as a writer of pure intellect and no body, apart from the flap photo Charlie eagerly masturbates to in the first half of the film. In Kaufman's fiction Laroche becomes Orlean's partner in crime (a role he is not unused to playing in his real life as a half-criminal person) and also loses his life. McKee's price is paid on another level, as a character assassination, and we shall return to his fate in connection with our specific examination of the use of satire in the script. These voluntary and involuntary sacrifices all go towards putting Charlie in a position where he can finish his screenplay in a serene state of mind, and perhaps also succeed in finding love and the meaning of life.

Textuality is ostentatiously illustrated throughout the film, most obviously through the numerous shots of characters reading, reading aloud (via voice over), or themselves producing texts via dictaphones, laptops etc. Many shots also simply feature text excerpts, for instance close-ups of highlighted passages from Orlean's book or from McKee's manual. Manuscripts are manifested as concrete objects passed from character to character in the film (and occasionally quoted by characters, or even in the credits portion of the paratext). Books and websites are shown frequently, particularly Orlean's and McKee's tomes, usually being read by Charlie and Donald. This saturation of textual representation in the film produces the mild meta-effect of mixing the diegetic levels, so that as viewers we are not always sure of the relationship between the image level and the narrated, told or read.

This sliding of levels can be illustrated by the following sequence 🎞: Susan Orlean is shown typing, we then hear her in voice over, presumably voicing the words we have just seen her typing. As this voice over occurs, the image level shifts to showing us the events she is narrating, namely Laroche driving down towards the orchid swamp he will soon be poaching orchids in. To complicate matters we then hear what appears to be a new voice-over talking about natural selection. This voice, however, is then revealed to be the sound of a tape deck in Laroche's van, featuring an audio recording of Darwin's writings. The various voice-overs are thus on different diegetic levels, but the viewer is disoriented by the slippage from level to level or narrative frame to narrative frame. The end result is that the story world of the film appears constructed out of various textual manifestations, grafted more or less subtly onto one another. We shall return to this in the section on palimpsesting.

Paratextual Markers as Meta-effects

The main paratextual phenomenon of interest to us in connection with the creation of meta-effects is of course the use of the title of the film itself. *Adaptation* is an obvious meta-reference to the process of adapting a text into a screenplay, and it is the process of doing just that that sets the frame for Charlie's progress (or lack thereof) throughout the movie. The word 'adaptation', however, has another equally important thematic resonance in the film, since the script flaunts a preoccupation with change, mutation, fitting in, and indeed, adapting to one's environment. This meaning of 'adaptation' also frames the Darwinian discourse we referred to above, and gives a context for the film's constant circling around the notion of evolution, mutation and change. Thus the orchid, as a particularly mutable and adaptable plant, functions as a conventional organizing symbol in the film's imagery (both in words and image), becoming almost the holy grail (particularly evident in Laroche and Orlean's quest for the 'ghost' orchid, later used for extracting the drug they become addicted to). Charlie, on the other hand, is contrasted to the orchid, and presented as a stubborn entity almost impermeable to mutation and adaptation, which might explain his difficulties in bringing his adaptation of Orlean's book to fruition. He, however, also ends up finding the grail substitute, when he adapts sufficiently (to Hollywood standards, to conventions, to easy solutions) to finish his adaptation. Paradoxically, he can only attain this goal when he abandons the notion of just writing 'about flowers' and returns to the 'artificially plot driven' (Kaufman 2002, p.5) formula of genre writing.

All films employ a type of paratext called credits. These may be shown at the beginning or end of a film (occasionally they are embedded after an initial sequence or prelude of the film has been run). Conventionally the credits have been generically marked off from the diegetic (usually fictional) world(s) of the film, and the viewing contract surrounding the credits is that the information presented in them is factual. Metafilms, however, have exploited the potential for slippage between fiction and fact in this conventional contract, and *Adaptation* takes this practice to new heights.

The credits to *Adaptation* end with a reference to Donald Kaufman, who, as mentioned above, dies in the film's diegetic world. When the credits read as their very last entry, 'In Loving Memory of Donald Kaufman' (Kaufman 2002, p.100), immediately following a quote from Donald's screenplay *The Three* (which we recognize from the film's plot as belonging to the fictional world), we as audience are confused, since this dedicatory practice is normally reserved for real dead people (usually people who have passed away in, or at least during, the process of filming of the movie in question). Since Donald Kaufman has also received co-screenwriting credits, both in the film version and the printed 'shooting script', the confusion is further aggravated. His fan site on the World Wide Web, Charlie Kaufman and Spike Jonze's reluctance to state unequivocally that Donald does not really exist, and, most bizarrely, Donald's nomination for an Academy Award are all factors contributing to the play surrounding Donald's status as somewhat more than just a fictional character. He is in fact similar to the type of entity we in metafiction, following Waugh, term a 'paper author'. This making 'real' of characters from the film's fictional register adds strongly to the film's ludic meta-character. The opposite process, the 'fictionalizing' of real, i.e. actual, people in the film is then experienced as a consequence also brought into a state of flux by the unexpected backwash of 'reality' through the film's diegetic levels. We are thus forced to wonder how 'real' the depiction of characters such as Orlean, Laroche, McKee and Valerie (who we know all have actual living correlatives) is, even when our common sense tells us that they are not really eaten by alligators or available on porn sites outside the film's diegesis.

We turn now to a rather specialized area of paratext, which can be used to contribute to the game of 'real fictitiousness' the filmmakers and distributors are playing with us as viewers. This is the feature of chapter titles, which is only operative in the DVD-version of films as commodity/art-product. One particular such chapter title in *Adaptation* warrants comment.

Chapter 27 is titled 'Deus Ex Machina', and in this chapter Donald's death in a car chase is depicted. The theme of *deus ex machina* as an unacceptable technique for creating a satisfactory ending to an otherwise unsolvable plot knot has already been raised in Charlie's conversation with McKee after his

Story seminar, where the screenwriting guru thunders, 'Find an ending. But don't cheat. And don't you dare bring in a *deus ex machina*' (McKee 1997, p.70). However, the only way Charlie can wrest back control of the screenplay after Donald has been brought in to help him (by following McKee's '10 Commandments' (McKee 1997, p.52)) is to kill him off in the diegetic world of Donald's own adaptation of Charlie's screenplay. This, by way of the permeable membranes between diegetic worlds in the film, will also kill Donald on the other levels in and outside the film (viz. the dedication in the credits), and Charlie as the only remaining Kaufman will be able to wrap up the writing.

A further jest in connection with the phrase *deus ex machina* is, of course, that Donald has become a god-like character in the movie at this point (having, as if by magic, scored a pretty girlfriend and a six-figure sum for his screenplay; having followed, Moses-like, McKee's '10 Commandments' to the letter; and having manipulated like a ruthless demigod the Orlean and Laroche characters), so he is literally the 'deus' of the phrase. The jest is completed by the fact that the way Donald dies is in fact by a literal ejection 'ex machina' as he is flung through the windshield of the brothers' car when Charlie rams another vehicle trying to flee from the suddenly murderous pair of Orlean and Laroche. Thus the paratext on the DVD version draws the viewer's attention to a pun, which may go undetected by the viewer in the cinema, who does not have the caption to jog his recognition of the joke being played on us (and McKee).

Palimpsesting and Other Intertextual Strategies

The most obvious palimpsesting in the film is the writing over of Orlean's original text, *The Orchid Thief*. The second layer of palimpsesting that is performed is that McKee's manual of screenwriting, *Story*, is used as a key to how to do the first palimpsesting (although Charlie refuses to adhere to these 'principles' in the early parts of the film, Donald then implements them all in 'his' part of the adaptation process, and finally Charlie, after regaining control of the script, keeps most of the McKeesque features intact, but as acts of defiance allows himself the use of the *deus ex machina* ending and extensive use of voice over).

Adaptation as Adaptation

Adaptation and *The Orchid Thief*

The Orchid Thief is indeed a hard book to adapt. While it contains a skeletal plot, there is almost no conflict in this plot, and the tensions between narrator and characters are subtle to the point of invisibility. Orlean stays aloof from her subject matter, yet is not averse to the occasional lyrical *tour de force*, as in the chapter 'Orchid Fever', which also helps Charlie provide the raw material for his failed attempt at picking up the friendly waitress Alice (DVD, chapter 11; Kaufman 2002, pp.32-33).

While there is a strong tone of reverence on Charlie's part for Orlean's style and specific formulations, which he quotes and accepts as valid credos (for instance, that orchids are suitable metaphors for life and love, being as Orlean states, 'A little fantastic and fleeting and out of reach', or in Charlie's paraphrase, 'God's miracles', (Kaufman 2002, p.70)), he gradually begins to doubt both her style and the validity of her claims – not to mention the possibility of adapting her 'storyless' book into any kind of Hollywood film. When pleading with his agent to get him off the hook by canceling the contract for the screenplay, Charlie first complains about the book's lack of story (this is reiterated in his confession to McKee later), but in this conversation Charlie also tries to palm off Laroche's dictum, mediated by Orlean's text, as his own credo: 'Show people how amazing flowers are' (Kaufman 2002, p.51). When Marty challenges this claim, which slightly more sensitive interlocutors such as Valerie have previously accepted at face value (perhaps because they recognize them as Orlean-quotes), by saying, 'Are they amazing?', Charlie flounders, 'I don't know. I think they are' (Kaufman 2002, p.51).

This doubt is a reflection of his chronic self-doubts, but not just that. It also feeds into his general mistrust of 'life lessons' (Kaufman 2002, p.5) which he has stated in the very early conversation with Valerie, where Charlie presents a model of screenwriting which no-one but him can really see the merits of: 'I'd want to let the movie exist, rather than be artificially plot driven' (Kaufman 2002, p.5). Orlean's occasionally smug, glib superior tone has not been noticed yet by Charlie at this early stage in the process, but his suspicion and eventual contempt of it evolves as he and Donald take turns at peeling off the layers of niceness that Orlean's writing persona projects in her text.

As the adaptation process evolves (or devolves) Charlie takes liberties with Orlean's book (with the help of Donald, who in turn almost ghost writes for McKee). Some elements remain unchanged (literally read aloud or shown as text), some are strongly adapted, some are altered beyond recognition (for instance what Charlie calls Orlean's ending in his conversation with McKee), and some entirely new elements are gratuitously added on (especially stock genre elements, such as man eating alligators, or the 'Swamp Ape', which unfortunately was written out of the script in the final draft). The so-called ending of Orlean's text (the already cited 'fantastic and fleeting and out of reach' (Kaufman 2002, p.70)) is in fact a quite early passage in her book (Orlean 1998, p.48), which is placed close to the end of a chapter, but exactly 300 pages away from the actual end of the book. Thus Charlie exaggerates the lack of story in Orlean's book to make the point of highlighting the difficulty of his adaptation process. An interesting sidebar is that in the earliest version of the screenplay, Kaufman lets Charlie quote the actual ending of Orlean's book to McKee in this scene, so we know that the change must have been inserted to add to the impression the viewer is supposed to get of Orlean's work as storyless.

Much of the story that actually ends Orlean's book is however also represented in the film, since these are the passages where Laroche and Orlean enter the swamps and get lost and have to leave without ever finding the ghost orchid. These passages are quite filled with narrative events and a form of suspense (will they find their way out?), so Orlean has in fact produced a form of conventional plot climax to end her text. The adaptation of *The Orchid Thief* in *Adaptation* is therefore not only selective, intrusively re-organizing and manipulative as most adaptations are, but clearly tendentious with a clear parodic intent as we shall explore below.

Adaptation and *Story* by Robert McKee

The beginning of the film/'shooting script' blatantly violates all of McKee's 'principles' ('A rule says, "You must do it *this way*". A principle says, "This works..."' (McKee 1997, p.3)), set forth in *Story*. After Charlie falls into the hands of a McKee-trained Donald, the script follows McKee's '10 commandments' to the letter (alternately this segment can be interpreted as Donald literally writing the screenplay from the point onward where Charlie asks for his help – we, however, never actually see Donald typing passages of the screenplay), and all goes horribly wrong until Donald is ejected from the film (through the car window), and a now strangely altered Charlie can finish the script, complete with 'profound life lessons' (Kaufman 2002, p.5). We actually reach a very high level of mock-pathos when Charlie starts quoting Donald's 'wisdom': 'Donald says: "That was her business, not mine. You are what you love, not what loves you. I decided that long ago".' (Kaufman 2002, p.98). These are the very words Donald uttered a few pages earlier in the screenplay, making Charlie 'cry softly', just before their moment of brotherly male bonding is interrupted by Orlean and Laroche almost finding and killing them (Kaufman 2002, p.93). We shall return to comment on this odd mock-pathos.

The segments where Charlie struggles alone without 'principles' exhibit numerous breaches of good practice according to McKee. In Chapter 15 of Story, 'Exposition', McKee holds forth on the theme of 'Show, Don't Tell' (1997, p.334). The basic tenets boil down to 'Skill in exposition means making it invisible. […] In other words, *dramatize exposition*' (1997, p.334). Thus, narration, especially of the psychologizing kind, should be kept to a minimum: 'We must realize that a screenplay is not a novel. Novelists can directly invade the thoughts and feelings of characters. We cannot. Novelists, therefore, can indulge in the luxury of free association. We cannot' (McKee 1997, p.343). Additionally, two techniques should be eschewed at almost all costs: the use of flashback and the use of voice over. On flashbacks McKee says, 'Rather than boring the audience with long, unmotivated, exposition-filled dialogue passages, we could bore it with unwanted fact-filled flashbacks' (1997, p.341). Both choices are equally bad in McKee's world, where the audience is king. On the topic of voice over his tone is even graver: 'The trend toward using telling narration throughout a film threatens the future of our art. More and more films […] indulge in this indolent practice. They […] tie images together with a voice droning on the soundtrack, turning the cinema into what was once known as *Classic Comic Books*' (1997, p.344). Charlie's first act is of course prone to the use of monstrous flashbacks covering four billion and forty years (Kaufman 2002, p.4 and 41), totally undramatized and fact-filled. What is worse is in fact his use of triple tiers of voice over to facilitate the slipping from one diegetic level to another. Without voice over of this kind Charlie's entire script would be impossible. This explains his fearful response to McKee's God-like pronouncement at the screenwriting seminar: 'And God help you if you use voice over in your work, my friends! Kaufman looks up startled.

McKee seems to be staring directly at him' (Kaufman 2002, p.67). Charlie is therefore prone to collide with all of McKee's ideas in his practice, and Kaufman dramatizes this in the script by letting McKee come out victorious from their direct confrontation at and after the seminar. Later, of course Charlie gets the last word on voice over (delivered in voice over, naturally): 'Shit, that's voice over. McKee would not approve. How else can I share his thoughts? I don't know. Well, who cares what McKee says?'

In between we have the McKee contaminated segments of the film. These contain all the elements on the list of don'ts that Charlie has laid out in his first conversation with Valerie. The movie first and foremost becomes 'artificially plot driven', which is Charlie's crucial object of loathing (Kaufman 2002, p.5), but down to the last detail, Charlie violates all of his initial dictums: 'I just don't want to ruin it by making it a Hollywood thing. You know? Like an orchid heist movie or something, or, y'know, changing the orchids into poppies and turning it into a movie about drug running, you know?' (Kaufman 2002, p.5). All these things come to pass as the orchids become an object of criminal passion and desire, but also the specific raw material for a green powder, which is snorted cocaine-style by the crazed Orlean in the latter stages of the Hollywoodification of the movie's plot.

Further, Charlie states, 'I don't want to cram in sex or guns or car chases. You know? Or characters learning profound life lessons. Or growing, or coming to like each other, or overcoming obstacles to succeed in the end [...] life isn't like that' (Kaufman 2002, p.5-6). The specific plot elements he mentions all come to haunt the script towards the end, in memorable scenes of Meryl Streep playing a horny drug fiend version of Orlean, Streep/Orlean holding Charlie at gun-point, Laroche shooting Donald, and finally the fatal car chase that kills Donald. What is more, the inescapable fact is that Charlie is seen to 'grow', to learn 'life lessons', to come to love his brother, and to overcome his central obstacle, his writer's block. This seems to take on the force of a crucial message of the film, potentially contradicting the credo that at first we take not just to be Charlie's, but also a version of Orlean's and certainly Kaufman's artistic belief. Only by suggesting an uneasy tension between parody and wishful thinking on Kaufman's part can we sustain an interpretation of this apparent conversion on Charlie/Kaufman's part. McKee has an astute comment on this tension in the piece included in the 'shooting script' as an appendix (McKee 2002, p.131), where he categorizes

Kaufman as a Modernist hold-out, who avails himself of the postmodern poetics and filmic language, but deep down still believes in the role of the rogue genius, the inspired artist/outsider as social critic and reformer.

Adaptation and Kaufman's Fictional Autobiography

The viewer is left with a clear feeling that much of *Adaptation* draws on real-life anxieties Kaufman may have felt at the time. Critics and interviewers have corroborated this notion – see for instance Kaufman's statements to Keith Simanton at imdb.com: 'I was hired to adapt this book. I struggled with it. I lost my mind a bit. I became desperate. I decided to put myself in and that's what I did' (2003). Nevertheless, Kaufman's use of his 'autobiography' to focalize the 'storyless' book he was struggling with has at least two effects: one on the structure of the movie and its ensuing message, another on the real life repercussions of the movie for its 'real' characters (chiefly Kaufman himself, but potentially also Orlean, Laroche, McKee etc.).

Kaufman reduces the message of Orlean's book by reversing the process she uses in her book. Her basic technique is to quote the off-beat philosophy of the eccentric Laroche, run the quotes through her liberal humanist distillery of ideology, and subsequently serve them up as general philosophical insights that even New York intellectuals can subscribe to (this includes the delicate metaphoric ascriptions likening the qualities of orchids to humans). Kaufman, focalized through Charlie, takes the perspective the other way, showing that any philosophy has to be reduced to the consequences it has for the individual, flawed and frail human being to be of any value. The weak and insecure Charlie can only 'grow' through philosophy when it becomes banal and clichéd and local.

The effects on the 'real' personages behind the film are still hard to gauge – especially for the marginal characters like McKee and Laroche, who presumably only thrive on notoriety.[i] Orlean claims in a piece included in the 'shooting script' that she is privileged to have had her book adapted by Kaufman. She refrains from saying anything about the inclusion of herself as a character, doing things that certainly were not part of her book. In the concluding paragraph she labels Kaufman's work 'not being a literal adaptation of my book, but a spiritual one, something that has captured (and expanded on) the essential character of what the book, I hope, was about: the process of trying to figure out one's self, and life, and love, and the wonders of the world' (Orlean 2002, p.ix). Orlean seems not to have noticed the alterations in message and the parodic interventions of Kaufman into the message of her book.

Interviews with Kaufman and the director, and several articles in the media, have played up the notion that one can trace the real from the fictitious details in this effort at confession/autobiography (Prendergast 2003). Of course, it is a myth that such mapping can be done, and one might argue that it is a deliberately constructed myth which is precisely designed to add fuel to the mad artist mystique already surrounding Kaufman, while apparently pseudo-self-deprecatingly debunking that very mystique of the 'genius' and 'unique voice' Kaufman is billed as possessing. His own life seems to have only received added cache from the publication of this film.

Adaptation and the Hollywood Megatext of Genre Films

Once Donald is in full swing of tweaking Charlie's script into a 'Story', he avails himself of a full register of Hollywood genre clichés. Donald has learned from McKee (McKee 1997, pp.79-99) that one has to find one's genre and stick to it. (The barbed question: 'What is your genre, Charlie?' is left dangling in the air by this, as by all of Kaufman's scripts.) Donald's genre is the thriller, and he spares few of the tricks and stock trademarks of that genre in the eight chapters (chapters 20-27, by the DVD version's count) he rules over. We have car chases, crocodile bites, desperate hideouts from madmen pursuing the protagonists with guns, heart to heart confessions under the threat of imminent death, and not least brotherly bonding during death when Charlie attempts to keep Donald alive by singing Donald's theme song 'Happy Together' to him as he is slipping away. All these clichéd elements are culled from the megatext conventions of the thriller genre, and while they are lampooned they are also lovingly performed, styled and technically carried out to perfection according to Hollywood industry standards. Added together these 'life lessons' must be read as a parody of the standard Hollywood strategy of leaving the viewer with a warm fuzzy feeling and a vague notion of self-betterment attained.

Adaptation as Parody

Adaptation as Genre Parody and Satire of Hollywood Praxis

Kaufman's parody of the megatext of the thriller genre, which has been milked so extensively by Hollywood, seems to have the intention of satirizing all aspects of the Hollywood practice of pasteurizing available texts, using them as grist for the mill of adaptation. McKee seems to be seen as the figurehead of the industry, and is an obvious target of Kaufman's satire. Valerie and Marty are other figures which are described as insensitive, money focused, success-driven yuppies without artistic integrity.

The chief locus of parody of the Hollywood megatext is, however, Donald's screenplay *The Three* which earns him a whopping fee (and high praise from Marty). This is a thoroughly McKeeish screenplay, but equally obviously a horrible piece of work when seen from the point of view of artistic merit and logical plausibility. The premise of Donald's script is hackneyed in the extreme, involving mass murder, other violence, sex, etc. Donald is convinced that he has attained artistic integrity, putting in a metaphoric colour scheme in the movie, adding a subtext about the dichotomy between technology and nature. The triviality of these techniques and ideas never occurs to Donald, but makes Charlie groan with embarrassment.

Adaptation as Parody of Orlean's Book

Despite repeated statements about how profound, true, and full of sad insights Orlean's book appears to Charlie, there seems to be a clear effort to parody, not only Orlean's life of quiet desperation but also the neatness and self-satisfied smugness of her text. Charlie has an outburst to McKee where he complains that the book has no story, and this of course makes it impossible to adapt. The finished film, on the extra-diegetic level we watch it, could also not have existed without an inserted extraneous story. That we get two extra stories, both that of Charlie's own desperate existence and that of Donald's warped potpourri of Hollywood clichés, would seem to indicate that Orlean's text is sorely lacking in more ways than one.

The parody extends to the comments Kaufman puts into the Orlean character's mouth at the end of the film: 'I did everything wrong. I want my life back. […] I want to be a baby again. I want to be new. I want to be new' (Kaufman 2002, p. 97). This desire towards infantility is similar to Charlie's own desire in the beginning and throughout large parts of the movie: 'Life is short. I need to make the most of it. Today is the first day of the rest of my life… I'm a walking cliché' (Kaufman 2002, p.1). Thus the plot loops back on itself, much like the Ourobouros figure Charlie accurately names, when Donald describes the snake tattoo his girlfriend has. Charlie compares himself to an Ouroborous, because he has written himself into the script, eating his own tail, potentially losing his identity in the process. Certainly this is what seems to have happened towards the end where Charlie/Kaufman lets Donald's theme, 'Happy Together', be sung by the Turtles, as the end credits begin to roll, and the world again speeds up in a stop-motion animation of morning glories opening and closing, signifying another circle of evolution and adaptation to the conditions of the world. Charlie has become a simpleton, child-like and hopeful. This outcome must be read as an opening towards self-parody in the film.

Adaptation as Self-parody (Three Different Scripts)

The final, dizzying twist to the layers of parody consists in Kaufman making available at least three different script versions, illustrating the development of the adaptation process itself. In doing so, Kaufman also offers us a view of the process of self-parody these script changes illustrate. There are overt comments on Charlie's previous scripts (which seem to be completely identical to Kaufman's production), so we already know that Charlie is wary of 'repeating himself'. Kaufman seems to have had fewer compunctions, allowing not only the overt quotes from *Being John Malkovich*, but also re-using some of his trademark techniques, such as monstrous flash-backs, speeded-up camera and other 'trick photography'. The confession in this movie that 'God, I've written myself into the screenplay' (Kaufman 2002, p.60), only makes explicit what has implicitly been the case in all the other screenplays Charlie/Kaufman has ever produced.

Specific elements of *Adaptation* must be classified as self-parodic. The notion that not only Donald's screenplay, but also Charlie's script use trite techniques and themes, deserves notice. When Charlie lectures Donald about the weakness of his ideas for *The Three*, he states, 'The only idea more overused than serial killers is multiple personality' (Kaufman 2002, p.31). Although Donald's script takes the idea to absurd extremes, folding the killer, victim and cop into one character, Kaufman's script is not far behind: Charlie and Donald being twins lets itself be read as them being two sides of the same character, which is close enough to abusing the notion of multiple personalities. The twin theme is overdetermined by being mentioned several times in the film, for instance by letting McKee mention twice that the screenwriters of *Casablanca* were also twins (Kaufman 2002, p.71). Furthermore, the extensive use of palimpsesting in connection with the set of voices represented in the movie smacks of holism – a theme which is further accentuated by the use of one specific quote from Donald's script as epitaph for him and as post-script to the whole movie. All the voices melt into one life lesson, much in the same way as 'Cassie' says in *The Three*, 'We're all one thing. [] Like cells in a body' (Kaufman 2002, p.100). The unity of the characters in *The Three* colours the perception of the characters in *Adaptation*, leading us to suspect self-parody in the case of the latter.

Since there are three versions of the screenplay available to the general public (the so-called 'second draft', dated September 24, 1999; the 'revised' version, dated November 21, 2000; and finally the 'shooting script', dated 2002), it is possible to investigate the development in the mock-pathos and self-parody of Kaufman's various endings. The earliest version seems the most self-indulgent. This version ends with a flash-forward ('Five billion and forty years later') where we witness the end of the world. The pretentiousness continues with a Shakespeare quote (not sourced, but from *Julius Caesar*, act 1, scene 2): "'Let me have men about me that are fat; Sleek-headed men and such that sleep o' nights'" (Kaufman 1999, p.117), followed by the familiar dedication to Donald Kaufman. Obviously this ending has less of the parodic slants, since it does not draw the focus very tightly to the role of Donald as teacher of Charlie's life lessons (Shakespeare has too big a role, so to speak), and since the closing of the creation/end, flashback/flash-forward circle is far too neat.

The revised 2000 version has inserted the Donald quote from *The Three* and retains the dedication, but does not indicate the use of The Turtles' song on the soundtrack. We also note that Orlean's character shoots herself in this script, while the movie version does not tell what end she comes to. It seems that particular event was too blatant a spelling out of Charlie (and Kaufman's) loathing of Orlean, but leaving it out makes it harder to detect the parody of Orlean in the 'shooting script'. Furthermore, the lack of The Turtles' song makes it harder to detect the running joke about turtles, which is established through the references to Laroche's habit of serial collecting of animals and objects, including turtles.

Finally, the ending of the 'shooting script' spells out the 'happy' part of the ending more than any of the previous drafts, thanks to Charlie's voice over: 'Kaufman drives off from his encounter with Amelia, filled for the first time with hope. I like this. This is good' (Kaufman 2002, p.100). What is Charlie assessing here? The quality of the script he is rushing home to type, or the 'real' life situation he is beginning to find himself in? If it is the latter, there is a certain smugness at having lost Donald and McKee in one fell swoop, and the viewers must contemplate the possibility that we are being shown (not told!) that Charlie is an asshole (his favourite epithet for Donald). If, rather, he is totally wrapped up in the process of finishing his script, the constructedness of the whole film is brought back into focus, and the audience must realize that Donald's death is merely the necessary *deus ex machina* Charlie needed to complete the script. This latter interpretation points to the multiple ironic and self-ironic layers of Kaufman's stimulating, but self-indulgent film.

REFERENCES

Genette, G. (1997a) *Palimpsests: Literature in the Second Degree.* Lincoln: University of Nebraska Press.

Genette, G. (1997b) *Paratexts: Thresholds of Interpretation.* Cambridge: Cambridge University Press.

Kaufman, C. (1999) *Adaptation*, BeingCharlieKaufman.com, URL (consulted June 2005): http://www.beingcharliekaufman.com/adaptation.pdf

Kaufman, C. (2000) *Adaptation*, BeingCharlieKaufman.com, URL (consulted June 2005): http://www.beingcharliekaufman.com/adaptationnov2000.pdf

Kaufman, C. (2002) *Adaptation: The Shooting Script.* London: Nick Hern.

McKee, R. (1997) *Story: Substance, Structure, Style and The Principles of Screenwriting.* New York: Regan Books.

McKee, R. (2002) 'Critical Commentary', in C. Kaufman Adaptation: *The Shooting Script*, pp.131-135. London: Nick Hern.

Orlean, S. (1998) *The Orchid Thief.* London: Vintage.

Orlean, S. (2002) 'Foreword', in C. Kaufman *Adaptation: The Shooting Script*, pp.vii-ix. London: Nick Hern.

Parker, I. (2003) 'The Real McKee', *The New Yorker*, 10 October. URL (consulted June 2005): http://www.newyorker.com/fact/content/?031020fa_fact

Prendergast, G. (2003) 'Truth and Fiction in Charlie Kaufman's *Adaptation*', Cyber Film School. URL (consulted April 2003): http://www.cyberfilmschool.com/articles/adaptation.htm

Simanton, K. (2002) 'IMDb Interviews Charlie Kaufman, Spike Jonze and Nicholas Cage', IMDb. URL (consulted December 2003): http://us.imdb.com/NewsFeatures/adaptation.html

Waugh, P. (1984) *Metafiction: The Theory and Practice of Self-conscious Fiction.* London: Routledge.

FILMS REFERENCED

Jonze, S. (dir.) (1999) *Being John Malkovich*. USA: Propaganda Films/Single Cell Picture.
Gondry, M. (dir.) (2001) *Human Nature*. USA: Fine Line Features.
Jonze, S. (dir.) (2002) *Adaptation*. USA: Columbia Pictures.
Clooney, G. (dir.) (2002) *Confessions of a Dangerous Mind*. USA: Miramax Films.
Gondry, M. (dir.) (2004) *Eternal Sunshine of the Spotless Mind*. USA: Focus Features.

WEB

Sony Pictures Digital, Inc. (2003) Official Web Page of the film *Adaptation*. USA: Sony Pictures. URL (consulted May 2005): http://www.sonypictures.com/homevideo/adaptation-superbit/index.html

Unknown (2001) BeingCharlieKaufman.com. URL (consulted June 2005): http://www.beingcharliekaufman.com

Unknown (2003) The Original Donald Kaufman Fan Club. URL (consultd May 2005): http://movies.groups.yahoo.com/group/donald_kaufman_fans/

NOTES

[i] However, McKee claims to have had mixed feelings about being a real fictitious character in Kaufman's screenplay: "In the movies of our own lives, McKee argues, we can take the role of protagonist. ('Have you ever been in love?' he asks. 'The day you met that person, that was an inciting incident.') But three years ago, when McKee was sent Charlie Kaufman's screenplay for *Adaptation*, he had a glimpse of another possible (and gloomier) truth: that in the movies of other people's lives we are lucky to get anything better than the role of a character actor, who, with a bundle of evident virtues and vices, bounces for a moment or two off the protagonist. 'I got this phone call in the middle of the day from New York, a very embarrassed producer,' McKee remembered. 'He said, 'This is the most embarrassing phone call I've ever had to make. I don't know how to say this, but there's this guy Charlie Kaufman, who did *Being John Malkovich*, and he's written this new screenplay, and he's quoted freely from your book and lecture without copyright permission, and we don't know what to do.' He needed McKee's permission. McKee read the script, and asked the opinion of two people: one was his friend William Goldman, the screenwriter and author of *Adventures in the Screen Trade*. 'Don't do it,' Goldman said. 'Don't fucking do it. It's Hollywood, and you can't trust them.' McKee then called his son, Paul, who is twenty-five. 'He said, 'Do it.' I said, 'But suppose they make fun of me?' He said, 'Dad, you're going to be a character in a Hollywood film.' McKee asked for two changes to the script. He wanted a 'redeeming scene,' and he was given it: an Obi-Wan Kenobi moment, in a bar, between his character and the Charlie Kaufman character. McKee also wanted a better ending. Although McKee does not quite see it this way, the joke of *Adaptation*'s final scenes is that, after Charlie Kaufman hears McKee lecture, the impulses of dumb blockbuster writing – sex and murder – take over the movie. McKee says that, in real life, he was trying to fix it. 'I said, 'Before I can consent, we have to have meetings. You have serious third-act problems.' McKee laughed - a loud 'ha!' – remembering that in earlier versions there was a character called the Swamp Ape, 'who came roaring out of the swamp and killed the Chris Cooper character.' McKee killed the Swamp Ape. As he told *Adaptation*'s producers, echoing the hope of redemption that runs through the heads of McKee's Story students, 'I cannot be a character in a bad movie. I can't be.'" (Parker, 2003) McKee thus cannot relinquish his desire to fix Kaufman's bad screenplay habits, but runs the risk of being ridiculed by the portrayal Kaufman gave of him in the selfsame screenplay.

Adapting Emotions in *The Hours*

Steen Christiansen

The Hours, as both novel and film, depends on a strong emotional narrative, in many ways specifically focused on the identification established between the three main characters and the reader/spectator. In order to investigate this further, I will examine the concept of how the narration is mediated into the cinematic medium, which will inevitably lead to a discussion of cinematic narration, particularly with regards to impersonal narration.

In this, I wish to engage in what Brian McFarlane calls enunciation (McFarlane 1996), but which I shall continue to call narration, though specifically in the area which Genette terms mood (Genette 1983). In doing so, I wish to distance myself from the narratologists who believe that there is such a thing as a non-narrator, that events in a text can somehow 'tell themselves'. I recognise the differences when speaking specifically of film, and I will concede that it may be less obvious to locate the narrator in a film, but that does not mean narration is not present.

When I have presented my argument for impersonal narration rather than a non-narrator, I shall examine the relations between tone, mood and the emotions of the text, and how these are communicated to the reader/spectator. While not specifically a cognitive reading, I will employ Torben Grodal's (1999) concepts of emotive narration from his article 'Emotions, Cognitions, and Narrative Patterns in Film'. This will enable me to focus on how narration may become emotive. Having presented Grodal's arguments, I shall proceed into analysing the emotive effects in connection with *The Hours* specifically, examining how emotive narration is transferred from novel to film. In this examination, I will specifically focus on how visual narration can evoke tone in the same way that written language can. I will try to show how this is done through the use of *mise-en-scene* and cinematography.

It should perhaps be noted here that I am not trying to 'overdetermine' film as compared to novels. I shall not argue that film can do everything novels can and more, but rather that emotional narration is not limited to the written medium and not dependent on a specific omniscient narrator which has access to the inner thoughts of the characters. On the other hand, I do believe that inner thought is at best clumsily done in the film medium, unless it is handled in symbolic ways, but we shall return to that.

Re-Locating Narration in Cinematic Adaptation

Whenever discussing the place of the narrator in a text, it is useful to remember, as Genette (1983) has specified, that all narration is by definition first person; it is simply a matter of whether the first person will be used to designate one of the characters in the text or not. The real question comes when one asks who controls the narration. Branigan argues that 'there is no consciousness of a narrator to produce (originate) sentences which then control meaning for a reader but exactly the reverse: the systematic restrictions perceived by the reader within a text are simply labeled as "narration" in order to be located when needed in the logical process of reading' (1986, p.59). This argument points to the fact that it is the reader, rather than the text itself, who creates a narration. While this may make sense to some extent, it seems to me that what is labelled 'narration' in the above quotation is nothing more than an implied narrator, which is still dependent upon cues in the text in order to be created by the reader. As such, there remains a narrating function, even if it is not specifically in control. This notion of control probably deals with the anthropocentric notion of the narrator. Bordwell argues that 'in watching films we are seldom aware of being told something by an entity resembling a human being [...] Most films do not provide anything like such a definable narrator, and there is no reason to expect they will. [...] Narration is better understood as the organization of a set of cues for the construction of a story. This presupposes a perceiver, but not any sender, of a message' (1985, p.62). What is so problematic about Bordwell's proposition is that he presents a communication model without a sender, which is in essence an incomplete communication model. If we agree that most texts are communicative, and that only the most avant-garde texts would attempt no communication, it becomes evident that we need a sender. This might be extremely difficult, if not impossible, to pinpoint, but that does not mean that it is not there. If nothing else, it must certainly exist as a function in the text, even if it is a function merely ascribed by the reader or the spectator.

I have no problem accepting that the narrator is to some extent created by the reader/spectator as some form of authority, or truth-establishing point, but I cannot accept that we can have a text without some form of sender. The problem is that we tend to conflate narrator with a person. As Ryan points out, 'The concept of narrator is a logical necessity of all fictions, but it has no psychological foundation in the impersonal case. This means that there is no need for the reader in impersonal narrations to seek an answer to the question "who speaks"?' (1981, p.519). It is this position of the 'who' which may suggest that a narrator need be a person, but as Roland Barthes has argued, 'A narrative is never made up of anything other than functions: in differing degrees, everything in it signifies' (1977, p.89). As we can see here, there is no particular reason for expecting the narrator to be a person. Even if the narrator doubles as a character, the character must be said to be a function. Clearly, the text as object has a sender in the form of an author, which must clearly exist. Bordwell, however, seems intent on getting rid of the author as the authority in the text, and so argues too hurriedly that a narrator is not necessary. There is always an author and an implied author, but even if there is only a narrating function, the narrative discourse must be structured by this same narrating function. What is so problematic about the narrator or narrating function is that it furthermore carries the notion of truth-function. That is, we tend to judge a narrator as being reliable or unreliable, ironic or serious and so forth, aspects which are all very human and certainly dependent upon what Genette calls the mood of narration. However, these aspects remain functions and are not dependent on having an anthropomorphic narrator which is also a diegetic or non-diegetic character.

It is here that we shall focus our attention, but in a particular way. If we have an impersonal narrator, how does that converge with emotional narration? Emotions, of course, can only be present in the reader/spectator, not the text itself. While narration might be described through specific textual functions, emotions cannot. But how do we feel then, since we all feel when we read texts and watch films?

Excavating the Evocative:
Activating the Audience through Emotion

It is probably not an exaggeration to claim that most readers/spectators prefer texts which strongly activate mind and body. This should not be simply understood as tear-jerkers, but also thrillers, mysteries, action-adventure and similar films. Films to a large extent depend on these activations in order for the spectator to engage with the film, and the same can be said for novels. Emotions are strongly tied to narratives, a basic similarity between novels and films. This is because feelings and emotions are motivational forces, not simply for us as readers/spectators but also for the characters. It becomes especially important to have access to a character's emotions if we are to engage properly with that character.

Activations of feelings, however, are more important than just engaging with characters. It often becomes vital in order to properly understand the narrative itself. It is evident from this that a number of films do not fall unproblematically into this category. Many so-called art texts disrupt this simple flow of feelings and so make it difficult to engage emotionally with the film, forcing the spectator instead to focus on the more formal properties of the text, to read the text as a specific experiment with form rather than trying to narrate a particular story. One might consider some of William Burroughs's more extreme cut-up experiments, or one might consider Chris Marker's *La Jeteé*, a film consisting of a series of still photographs with no continuous action.

Works such as these do not carry an emotional flow, so to speak, but the flow is blocked (Grodal 1996, p.128). Popular genre adaptations, such as Stephen King thrillers and other mainstream films such as *Lord of the Rings* or *Cold Mountain* fall into the category of unblocked narratives where the emotional flow will typically lead to the solution of the narrative problem and so on to narrative closure. *The Return of the King* is a good example of how the conventions regarding unblocked emotional flow are difficult to disrupt without getting mixed results; because of the long-winded ending necessary in the process of adapting the books in good faith, people who did not know the books found it peculiar that the narrative continued when both emotional and narrative closure had taken place.

There are different levels of feelings defined by Grodal (1996, p.129) in the following way:

> # Vividness: the power of an isolated percept.
> # Salience: the percept in context.
> # Excitations: local activations linked to central human concerns, such as a kiss is usually romantic.
> # Emotions: activations linked to global narrative concerns, so that the percept takes on deeper meaning, such that the final kiss in *Four Weddings and a Funeral* is far more important than the earlier ones.

Mapping Emotions through Narrative Style

I will specifically deal with emotions for the rest of this article, though the others might come up as well. The emotional flow will be controlled by the aesthetic concerns of the work into a group of modal qualities (Grodal 1996, p.136), which are as follows:

> # Intense: vivid or salient percepts with non-narrative concerns.
> # Saturated: salient percepts that activate associations charged with affect.
> # Tense: percepts induce 'action-readiness'.
> # Emotive: percepts induces autonomic outlet (tears, laughter, shivers).

Narratives provide schemata which readers/spectators conceptualise and evaluate in relation to their knowledge of characters, genre, and other conventions. It is based on this that we comprehend the narrative. Genres use a variety of what we can call narrative and generic filters to activate specific emotions in the spectator from the narrative action. This may happen by either negating an emotion or creating an affective distance. Consider a woman getting ready for bed, whom we see through a window. This could both be the beginning of a romantic film, where the hero would sing beneath her window, or perhaps climb to her. It could also be the beginning of a slasher film where an insane killer is waiting for lights out to do his deeds. In order for the film to activate the proper emotions in the spectator, it has a number of choices, such as changes in music or reverse shots to establish who is standing beneath the window. The film may also choose to do neither, thereby creating an affective distance. Another way could be to create multiple foci of attention, such as for instance having more than one protagonist. But if spectators prefer emotional engagement with the narrative and the characters, and if an unblocked emotional flow is the best way to reach the audience, why ever choose an affective distance?

One answer could be to grant the text a specific status. Many melodramas and romantic films have absolutely no affective distance but use any cinematic device available to foster emotions in the spectator, including close-ups, visual filters, overlighting or underlighting, exceptionally dramatic music, persistently showing characters weeping or rejoicing in their love, wallowing in self-pity, and so forth. They are perhaps the best example of emotional insistency. But they are also often criticised for being the equivalent of emotional pornography, and condemned by critics for not being serious enough but rather indulging in the display of human emotions, as if great art must necessarily wear a stone face (Witness some performances of Shakespeare or Beckett, for instance.)

It does seem that if there is some form of 'serious' intention behind a text, then one must not indulge in emotional affect, but rather maintain a cool distance to what is portrayed, to present the narrative in an investigatory light where the human condition is examined. This is not meant to patronise the more serious texts which dwell on human condition, but it is in order to provide an understanding of the difference between the more mainstream approaches to emotional events and the more avant-garde approach. Here, I regard *The Hours,* both as novel and film, to be a more detached view of the tragic events it portrays than, for instance, *Philadelphia,* which also deals with a person dying of AIDS.

So, when speaking of blocked and unblocked narratives and emotional flows, we come across one instance which is specific for novels more than films, and that is the descriptive pause. Whenever a novel describes something from a third-person point of view, which is often regarded as a detached view with a maximum of truth value, then we have a descriptive pause, where the narrative clearly pauses. This descriptive pause can sometimes be extremely extended and even take over the central focus. When this happens, it is usually not appreciated and has been termed a 'purple patch', something D.H. Lawrence was often found guilty of. When the descriptive passage becomes too much, a purple patch, it is often because it takes on lyrical connotations, extending into poetry rather than remaining prose. This is slightly more difficult with regards to film, as every shot is description in addition to whatever else it is. As such, it is never entirely descriptive and because of this is cannot be classified as a descriptive pause. One can consider some more experimental films as one long descriptive pause, such as Andy Warhol's *Empire,* an eight-hour long film of the Empire State Building from one static position. Here, however, we might be reaching the limits of film itself. I do believe the camera can invoke tone. While the physical camera of course cannot invoke anything much, the shot can evoke plenty through the use of mise-en-scene and cinematography. It is here, I believe, that we can find what corresponds to the mood of narration, and it is what I will investigate further now.

The same three female characters are depicted in the novel, *The Hours,* and the film of the same title. Both formats employ a non-linear narrative structure that skips back and forth through the various time periods. This narrative fragmentation must be seen to carry at least some significance, a kind of discursive contiguity where actions take on significance because they are placed close together. It is also the place where we realise that the adaptation wishes to be more than a 'simple' mainstream film, since it does not rearrange the events into a proper causality, but chooses to follow the movement between different narrative times, as is the case with the novel.

When we look at what binds the text together across the different periods, we see that there are some central concerns which repeat and echo. For both the novel and the film this seems to be one way to avoid too much emotional indulgence, but also a way of making the considerations more universal, to deal with the similarities and differences of the period and the women. In this way the three characters of Virginia, Laura and Clarissa become three sides of the same woman, though Clarissa is somewhat reversed and is as much an echo of Leonard, being the one who tries to help the suffering poetic genius. A number of events are repeated but given different meanings due to different situations. On the other hand, we cannot help drawing connections between these repeated events and give them specific meaning according to their repetition. Specific, highly important events are the kisses between two women and the choices of death or life. Let us begin with the kisses. Laura's kiss comes as a form of consolation to Kitty:

> *Kitty nods against Laura's breasts. The question has been silently asked and silently answered, it seems. They are both afflicted and blessed, full of shared secrets, striving every moment. They are each impersonating someone. They are weary and beleaguered; they have taken on such enormous work.*
> *Kitty lifts her face, and their lips touch. They both know what they are doing. They rest their mouths, each on the other. They touch their lips together, but do not quite kiss.*
> *It is Kitty who pulls away.*
> *'You're sweet', she says.*
> *Laura releases Kitty. She steps back. She has gone too far, they've both gone too far, but it is Kitty who's pulled away first. It is Kitty*

whose terrors have briefly propelled her, caused her to act strangely and desperately. Laura is the dark-eyed predator. Laura is the odd one, the foreigner, the one who can't be trusted. Laura and Kitty agree, silently, that this is true. (Cunningham 1999, p.110)

While there is some eroticism to this kiss, mostly in the beginning with the brushing against the breasts, the situation quickly changes and becomes uncomfortable. The not-quite kiss becomes a transgression and Laura is portrayed as the transgressor.

In the film 💋, the kiss is emphasized with a close-up, following Laura as she pulls back. We can see from her expression that she is confused and we hear children playing in the background, an alien intrusion which destroys the intimacy of the moment, positioning the women as mothers rather than lovers. Kitty is filmed from above, with large eyes saying, 'You're sweet', as in the novel, making her seem almost a child, innocent and defenseless. This is the closest we get to Laura being the dark-eyed predator. What is added in the film, is Laura's question as Kitty is about to leave. 'You didn't mind?', answered by Kitty's 'What?', indicating that this will be something to be ignored, something which never happened. This underlines the transgression which Laura has committed but it needs to be verbalised in the film by the characters, since it would perhaps be too difficult to manage with purely visual information.

The kiss moves from an excitation which becomes saturated by importance, in that it takes on a symbolic meaning. The kiss becomes representative for Laura's wish to leave her domestic life behind and in that sense it becomes an emotional kiss. This is not necessarily easy to recognize by the spectator, hence the required add-on of Laura's question, to make the kiss take on meaning. We hear the hope in Laura's voice that perhaps she can get greater intimacy with Kitty from the kiss, but this is denied.

Virginia's kiss is similar to Laura's, as it also comes as a form of desire to escape from her home, the same domestic situation in which Laura is caught. However, there is a difference in the kiss's position from novel to film, and in the way it is used. In the novel Virginia and Vanessa sit while the maid Nelly cooks:

> *Here is Nelly with the tea and ginger and here, forever, is Virginia, unaccountably happy, better than happy, alive, sitting with Vanessa in the kitchen on an ordinary spring day as Nelly, the subjugated Amazon queen, Nelly the ever indignant, displays what she's been compelled to bring.*
> *Nelly turns away and, although it is not at all their custom, Virginia leans forward and kisses Vanessa on the mouth. It is an innocent kiss, innocent enough, but just now, in this kitchen, behind Nelly's back, it feels like the most delicious and forbidden of pleasures. Vanessa returns the kiss. (Cunningham 1999, p.154)*

As we can see, here the kiss is a stolen treasure, something wonderful and positive. Nelly is the incarnation of all society's rules which Virginia cannot cope with and loathes, everything she wants destroyed, everything normally deemed proper. Therefore, it becomes a victory when she can kiss her sister without Nelly discovering. It becomes an almost childish, playful thing, a secret kept from the real world, the world of propriety. It especially becomes a victory because Vanessa returns the kiss, so it is not dirty and a transgression as in Laura's case.

In the film, however, it feels different. Here the kiss is placed as Vanessa is leaving and Virginia forcefully kisses her, almost violently. It does not take on the transgressive nature of Laura's kiss, either, since Vanessa does not struggle and also kisses Virginia's fingers, but it is not a secret pleasure as in the novel. There is less emphasis on the kiss, we never see their lips meet, so it has little of the eroticism in it, which Laura's kiss did, instead it seems as an insistent outburst of emotion from Virginia, trying to force something from her sister.

In the film, it becomes a tense emotional scene, where Virginia's despair and desperation it placed in the foreground, while in the text we have more of an emotional emotive outlet, where we feel the same secret pleasure which Virginia does. In the novel, the kiss is a positive, beautiful thing because it helps Virginia. We can see how happy she is, but in the film it is accompanied by tears. Hereby, the film insists on drawing a more direct line to Laura's kiss as something which tries to break the bonds of society, to insist upon the similarities between Virginia and Laura.

If we turn to the other side of the breaking away from the life being led, we encounter a number of choices between life and death. Richard is the first we see choose death, although he is destined to die because of his illness. In Cunningham's text, we read:

> *The apartment is full of light. Clarissa almost gasps at the threshold. All the shades have been raised, the windows opened. Although the air is filled only with the ordinary daylight that enters any tenement apartment on a sunny afternoon, it seems, in Richard's rooms, like a silent explosion. Here are his cardboard boxes, his bathtub (filthier than she'd realized), the dusty mirror and the expensive coffeemaker, all revealed in their true pathos, their ordinary smallness. It is, quite simply, the tenement apartment of a deranged person. (1999, p.195)*

Notice how the film cannot represent a 'silent explosion' and instead lets Richard explode with reaction which is not present in the novel, where Richard simply sits on the windowsill. There is, however, a particular silence, which is that of the lack of music. The music ceases immediately when she enters and creates a more sombre emotional context rather than an overly dramatic score. The single piano comes in to signify the relevance of what Richard says. It slowly ambles along creating a rhythm to their conversation and turns into a flourish when Richard leaps from the window and we see him fall.

The scene's focus is placed on Clarissa, where there are close-ups of her but only close medium shots of Richard. This can be seen as the cinematic equivalent of creating a certain distance to Richard, while narrating Clarisa's emotions and feelings. This is parallel to what is done in the book, where we are only given access to Clarrisa's thoughts and not Richard's. This is further underlined with the shot of Clarrisa's face after Richard has fallen. We remain with her, only leaving her point of view for a more dramatic shot of Richard falling, one which symbolically blocks out our vision.

> *He inches forward, slides gently off the sill, and falls.*
> *Clarissa screams, 'No'–*
> *He seems so certain, so serene, that she briefly imagines it hasn't happened at all. She reaches the window in time to see Richard still in flight, his robe billowing, and it seems even now as if it might be a minor accident, something reparable. She sees him touch the ground five floors below, sees him kneel on the concrete,*

> *sees his head strike hears the sound he makes, and yet she believes, at least for another moment, leaning out over the sill, that he will stand up again, groggy perhaps, winded, but still himself, still whole, still able to speak. (Cunningham 1999, p.200)*

Here we have an example of what novels can do, or choose to do, which this film chooses not to do. The novel goes on to describe how Richard looks and describes how Clarissa runs to him and finds him covered in blood and lying on a broken beer bottle. While this could be shown on the screen, a choice must be made how to present Richard's body. The choice we see is that he simply falls and when his figure blacks out the screen, we see a horrified and shocked Clarissa and then a cut to the birthday cake of the Mrs. Brown storyline.

Considering other choices, we realise that there would be a choice between activating a strong autonomic, emotive outlet, by seeing Clarissa mourn Richard. In a more typical mainstream film, this would have happened with Clarissa crying over the dead body. The other option would be to choose a more intense and saturated association, trying to create a symbolic resonance in the death of Richard. A lingering shot on his body, even if it was done with subtle and subdued codes, emphasising the repercussions of the death, could too easily be seen as gross and exaggerated.

Instead, the film opts for contrast, moving directly to a close-up of the birthday cake, significantly keeping the theme of the music, not altering the flourishing piano but keeping it. We see how this contrast and the constant music creates some of the same effect which we get from Mrs. Brown's inner dialogue:

> *The candles are lit. The song is sung. Dan, blowing the candles out, sprays a few tiny droplets of clear spittle onto the icing's smooth surface. Laura applauds and, after a moment, Richie does too. 'Happy birthday, darling', she says.*
> *A spasm of fury rises unexpectedly, catches in her throat. He is coarse, gross, stupid; he has sprayed spit on the cake. She herself is trapped here forever, posing as a wife. She must get through this night, and then tomorrow morning, and then another night here, in these rooms, with nowhere else to go. She must please; she must continue. (Cunningham 1999, p.205)*

This emotion can be difficult to translate into film, and is done here through the contrast of death and birthday. Because the music continues rather than changing, it seems that we are invited to read this next scene in the same light. Rather than the literal death of Richard we have a symbolic death of Laura's love for her husband and her desire to get away from her situation. The effect is that in the film, when Laura leaves, it may come as a greater surprise than in the novel where we have constantly been presented with her inner thoughts. The film, on the other hand, is forced to share these thoughts some other way if it wishes to avoid the clumsy use of voice over narration, which might become especially problematic with three protagonists. For this reason there is a greater requirement of specific interpretive moves in order to realise what is happening; most of these moves depend on a specific symbolic reading of the film.

Laura considers death also. In the novel we have:

> *It is possible to die. Laura thinks, suddenly, of how she – how anyone – can make a choice like that. It is a reckless, vertiginous thought, slightly disembodied – it announces itself inside her head, faintly but distinctly, like a voice crackling from a distant radio station. She could decide to die. It is an abstract, shimmering notion, not particularly morbid. Hotel rooms are where people do things like that, aren't they? It's possible – perhaps even likely – that someone has ended his or her life right here, in this room, on this bed. Someone said, 'Enough, no more'; someone looked for the last time at these white walls, this smooth white ceiling. By going to a hotel, she sees, you leave the particulars of your own life and enter a neutral zone, a clean white room, where dying does not seem quite so strange.*
>
> *[...]*
>
> *She strokes her belly. I would never. She says the words out loud in the clean, silent room: 'I would never'. She loves life, loves it hopelessly, at least at certain moments; and she would be killing her son as well. She would be killing her son and her husband and the other child, still forming inside her. (Cunningham 1999, pp.151-152)*

Remediation Technique: Metafiction in Adaptation

The book explicates what she thinks about and all her inner discussions about killing herself. This is done through inner monologue, rather than describing actions. The film isolates Laura in the room, by using a tilted long shot. It also shows pills, and though there is no mention of that in the novel, this is the visual way of showing her thoughts on suicide. There is an inserted scene with the cake, visualising how this is central to her present thoughts, and of the book, which is the major alien element in Laura's life, the room of her own.

Here we encounter a weak metafictional aspect with the inter-cutting to Woolf's life and the comment that Virginia has two lives: her own and the life of her book. This seems to be the same with regards to Laura, who has made a room of her own from the book. It does seem that the book is the major reason for Laura being dissatisfied with her life. When Woolf says, 'It is possible to die', this breaks the narration from the novel which Laura is reading. As presented in the book, what the voice of Woolf narrates is also part of the novel until those words, which interrupt the narrative found in the text. With Woolf looking off-camera we almost feel as if she is seeing Laura in her bed twenty years later. This is a clear instance of frame-breaking where the two different narrative times converge to generate one specific effect.

Returning to the process of adapting the scene, we can see how the shift to Woolf's time creates narrative tension. Will Laura kill herself? At the time we might very well believe so, since she has seemed so unhinged for the better part of the film, and with the specific cues of the pills our initial expectation is indeed that. We experience another frame-break when water rises on the sides of Laura's bed, clearly not to be seen in a realistic light but instead in a symbolic light, as a metaphor for being swallowed and washed away. The frame-break comes specifically in the water, which echoes Woolf being swallowed in the beginning of the film. To conclude the metafictional sidetrack, we can see how the text forces us to parallelise between the two women, as we not done before.

Visually, however, we see how the water swallows Laura, complete with river plants and what not, so this is clearly the symbolic equivalent of the earlier water. The film parallels the two instances; it is at this point in the narrative that Laura's life changes from Woolf's. Both are caught in a life they do not like and want to escape. Both have escaped into the world of fiction and both feel that they are holding their husbands back. By not dying, Laura chooses a different route and this alters her situation. Instead of dying she leaves her husband and child, symbolically transferring the death to him many years later. She, however, might as well have been dead, which we shall see later. We can see how the tension of waiting for Laura to perhaps die is resolved but only through a saturated symbolic action. It will confuse a straight realist reading of the film to explain the water, and the water is also specifically added by the film, it is not present in the novel.

There is of course another death in the film which is important. It is also interesting to see how it is presented in the two media. Both begin with the death of Virginia Woolf but when the text ends, the novel revisits the death in this manner.

> *She nods. She will remain on good behavior, now that London's been decided on. She leaves the parlour, crosses the hall, and enters the darkened dining room. Long rectangles of moonlight mixed with street light fall through the window onto the tabletop, are swept away by windblown branches, reappear, and are swept away again. Virginia stands in the doorway, watching the shifting patterns as she would watch waves break on a beach. Yes, Clarissa will have loved a woman. Clarissa will have kissed a woman, only once. Clarissa will be bereaved, deeply lonely, but she will not die. She will be too much in love with life, with London. Virginia imagines someone else, yes, someone strong of body but frail-minded; someone with a touch of genius, or poetry, ground under by the wheels of the world, by war and government, by doctors; a someone who is, technically speaking, insane, because that persons sees meaning everywhere, knows that trees are sentient beings and sparrows sing in Greek. Yes, someone like that. Clarissa, sane Clarissa – exultant, ordinary Clarissa – will go on, loving London, loving her life of ordinary pleasures, and someone else, a deranged poet, a visionary, will be the one to die. (Cunningham 1999, p.211)*

Now, to me, it is impossible not to read this in a metafictional light, but specifically a double metafictional light. First of all, it seems that the deranged, visionary poet that needs to die in order for Clarissa to live is Virginia Woolf herself. It seems to be the only echoing we find in the novel of the death of Woolf, which occurs in the beginning. By conflating the two levels of the novel and her own life, Woolf moves into a typical metafictional strategy of blending fact and fiction. Michael Cunningham's novel itself seems to indicate this same shifting of levels, playing with the idea of Woolf committing suicide in order for one of her own characters to live. What is more interesting, however, is the way that we cannot help, as readers of Cunningham's novel, to draw connections between the first framed fictional Clarissa, the one in Woolf's novel, and the one we encounter in Cunningham's novel, the one called Clarissa Vaughn (but who Richard significantly calls Mrs. Dalloway). There is an interesting reversal of Clarissa's sexuality, since she is lesbian in Cunningham's novel but has kissed Richard once, reversing the events in Woolf's novel. Then we have the doubling of the events where Clarissa must lose someone close to her in order for her to go on living as a sane person. Here Richard dies, one who is certainly also a deranged poet and frail of mind. He is not strong of body, though, because doctors have broken him.

What is interesting is that there is a heterosexual woman in the story who experiences a lesbian kiss, and that is Laura Brown. This becomes the third metafictional level of the novel, where her reading Woolf's novel also seems to create a similarity between the events of her life and those of the novel. It is also Richard's death which must keep her lonely, but at the same time she has been lonely for a long time, being separated from Richard and also having left her husband. Again, the marriage seems to take on a symbolic life itself, being what must die so Laura can remain sane. She often considers how she feels trapped in her marriage and domestic life.

Here we see how the three different stories intertwine in a complex web of intertextuality and metafictionality. The use of contiguity invites this type of reading, but how does the film conversely deal with these levels? The short answer is that it doesn't. Rather than present the thoughts of Woolf, it chooses to intersperse the end of the novel with a return to the opening of the film and the death of Woolf. The disappearance of Woolf becomes the end of the film, so she is both the beginning and the end of the film, in a particular circular movement. The film seems to parallelise two women going to sleep with the death of Woolf. There seems to be no insistence on Laura and Clarissa dying, but rather a form of return to something positive. While Richard's death is a sad thing, it is also something which sets them free. This, I believe, is the reason for the return to Woolf's death.

Richard has been their Woolf and like Woolf to Leonard, Richard (to them) held them back, so that they could not live their own lives. In this way, the film chooses a more mainstream approach, not trying to question its own narrative voice, but rather depending on symbolism to close the story. Woolf's death becomes a double death, for when she dies, Richard dies properly from the lives of Laura and Clarissa, much in the same way as is made explicit in the novel:

> *It seems, at that moment, that Richard begins truly to leave the world. To Clarissa it is an almost physical sensation, a gentle but irreversible pulling-away, like a blade of grass being drawn out of the ground. Soon Clarissa will sleep, soon everyone who knew him will be asleep, and they'll all wake up tomorrow morning to find that he's joined the realm of the dead. (Cunningham 1999, pp.224-225)*

While the film decides to leave the metafictionality behind, it keeps the focus on how the emotions are transmitted. Any adaptation cannot help but being also a reading of the source material, yet what we can see is that films may choose to adapt emotions as well as narrative. This is done via various strategies in the use of mise-en-scene and cinematography, as well as more standard practices of adaptation, such as adding or removing dialogue and events. Emotion is therefore of vital importance when adapting novels into film.

REFERENCES
Barthes, Roland (1977) *Image-Music-Text*. Glasgow: Fontana Paperbacks.
Bordwell, D. (1985). *Narration in the Fiction Film*. Madison: University of Wisconsin Press.
Branigan, E. (1986) 'Point of View in the Fiction Film', *Wide Angle* 8(3-4): 4-52.
Cunningham, M. (1999) *The Hours*. London: Fourth Estate.
Genette, G. (1983) *Narrative Discourse: An Essay In Method*. Ithaca: Cornell University Press.
Grodal, T. (1999) 'Emotions, Cognitions, and Narrative Patterns in Film', in C. Plantinga and G. Smith (eds.) *Passionate Views: Film, Cognition, and Emotion*, pp.127-145. Baltimore: The Johns Hopkins University Press.
McFarlane, B. (1996) *Novel to Film: An Introduction to the Theory of Adaptation*. Oxford: Clarendon Press.
Ryan, M. (1981) 'The Pragmatics of Personal and Impersonal Fiction', *Poetics* 10: 517-539.

FILMS REFERENCED
Daldry, S. (dir.) (2002) *The Hours*. USA. Miramax Films.
Jackson, Peter (dir.) (2003) *The Lord of the Rings: The Return of the King*. USA. New Line Cinema.
Marker, Chris (dir.) (1962) *La Jeteé*. France. Argos Films.
Minghella, Anthony (dir.) (2003) *Cold Mountain*. USA. Miramax Films.

Medea Re-mediated

Ove Christensen

Lars von Trier's made for television film *Medea* was first broadcast on the national channel DR (Danish Broadcasting Corporation) Good Friday 1988, and it started an outcry from critics and viewers alike.[ii] The telephone lines were blocked at DR by viewers protesting about the programme and the daily's critics killed the film in reviews in the following day's papers. They rejected the film's lack of clearly defined sympathies and psychologically well-defined characters; they criticized as superficial the film's surrender to imaginary fascinations and its refusal to let a straight narrative and unambiguousness rule. Critics also attacked the telefilm's explicitness in showing a mother's killing of her own children as empty provocation, indicative of the film's symbolic shallowness. The Good Friday evening was a huge television night and more people were offended because they felt they were cheated of the light entertainment they expected for a pleasant evening with the family.

What made *Medea* even more provocative was that it was broadcast within the framework of 'television theatre', a label that guaranteed high quality culture for a broad audience. The 'television theatre' framework was understood by the broadcasters as part of the commitment to public service and the obligation to offer high culture to the general public regardless of education and social upbringing. At first 'television theatre' productions were nothing but filmed stage plays. Later on they took advantage of the possibility of moving the camera around and so aesthetically approached a more cinematic style of telling. The late 1960s and 1970s were a 'golden age' for Danish televised plays, and televised theatre still had a bearing in the 1980s before von Trier broke the tradition by using it for aesthetic experiments and avant-garde productions in violation of the tradition. Interestingly, numerous 'television theatre' productions depicted high modernist plays by the likes of Ionesco, Beckett and Pinter. These plays, however, were always transformed in a television language deprived of any abnormality whatsoever. The content might have been absurdist, the remediation, however, was anything but. The medium itself was taken as a 'natural' means for transmitting literary content to images that maximized transparency without influencing these images the slightest.

Diving deeper into the culturally informed reviews of von Trier's *Medea* it becomes evident that they are not just attacking the avant-gardism of the film's aesthetics. The real serious crime was twofold. Besides the replacement of the plot by the imagery – the first serious crime – von Trier abandoned the intrinsic values of Euripides' play and replaced them with his own idiosyncrasies and aesthetic taste. Not only was von Trier's *Medea* a violation of the tradition and 'genre' of 'television theatre' it was also a violation of the cultural heritage of classical European culture. This violation was itself doubled in that the Danish director Carl Th. Dreyer, who had become canonized at that time – at least within the academic and the cultural elites, originally wrote the script for the film *Medea*. According to the critics, Dryer's serene realism was violated by the film's insistent visual bravura and imagery. It was, however, primarily on the Greek dramatist's behalf that the reviewers protested. Euripides' *Medea* was 'strangled', as one reviewer put it.[iii] Another reviewer found consolation in the fact that Euripides' play had already survived for more than 2.000 years and so it would survive von Trier's (mis)take on it, even though this late take was killing all the real value in the play. Still another reviewer lamented that von Trier's *Medea* made an otherwise comprehensible play with a clear psychological conflict incomprehensible by turning the story aside for the indulgence in pure imagery. The television film deprived the original play of its intrinsic meanings, it was argued, by giving away the Aristotelian dramaturgy with its stress on the plot.

The most pervasive critique in the reviews decried the displacement of story and dialogue by pure imagery, seen as a lack of serious engagement in the psychological depth of characters and the theme of the play. These attacks illustrate how disappointed expectations when it comes to an adaptation of a classic text are articulated. The new *Medea* was covering for – or strangling – the old, more true and original *Medea*, staged in Athens in 431BC. And perhaps worse, this displacement was not even entertaining and funny but presumptuous and burdened by shallow pathos, it was claimed.

Reviewers accustomed to television plays that adopt the logic of the naturalistic theatre did not know what to make of von Trier's experiment with the form of television and its fusing of techniques from television, video and film. The different techniques were mixed to a new composite art form visually more like music videos than easily digested high culture. They expected a *translation* or *transmission* from one medium to another, or perhaps more precisely a mere paraphrase of the play as in filmed stage theatre. Therefore, they did not acknowledge the attempt to investigate the visual potentials of the television medium itself. The displacement of theatricality by the composite of television, cinematic and video techniques was interpreted as a failure and made the film scholar Dan Nissen claim that it was obvious from the experiment that von Trier did not want to make the film in the first place. Nissen concluded that von Trier 'is out of touch with the energetic layers in Euripides' text'.[iv] He concluded that von Trier reduced Euripides' play to an act of pure provocation without any bearing on the original.[v]

The reviewers' hostile reception of *Medea* proved the notion of a conservative stance within the cultural elite right. The cultural establishment, represented by the elitist reviewers, saw themselves more as keepers of the good (learned) taste than critics relating to a current cultural expression. They supported the 'museolization' of culture instead of supporting a living culture. The sacrosanct play of Euripides was not to be toyed with by a proclaimed visionary filmmaker without authorization – and authorization is the key here. Euripides was imagined as the 'author' and the reviewers saw themselves as the custodial priesthood guarding the legacy of the cultural values passed down through the centuries. Their perspective appears to assert a solitary author who creates an 'original' that can only circulate through history if kept in its pure form; it can be transmitted but not influenced. These elite recognize the eternal value of the play in its essence, and this essence can only be maintained by an innermost obedience toward the inherent significance of the work.

But, instead of keeping a work alive by installing it in a museum, the keepers are really only celebrating its death by protecting it from contemporary interpretations. The German art philosopher Theodor Adorno argues that the museums incarcerate works of art and in the end art will suffocate and eventually die from this treatment:

> *The German word museal [museumlike] has unpleasant overtones. It describes objects to which the observer no longer has a vital relationship and which are in the process of dying. They owe their*

> *preservation more to historical respect than to the needs of the present. Museum and mausoleum are connected by more than phonetic association. Museums are the family sepulchres of works of art. (Crimp 1983, p.49)*

If the viewers and reviewers expected an easy transformation of Euripides' play, it is no surprise that they were shocked. The reason for the rejection of von Trier's *Medea* may be manifold but that the reviewers were taken aback by the televisual experiment is at least part of an explanation. The surprise was that *Medea* was supposed to be dead and the corpse well known. The revitalization of *Medea* was only understood as a desecration of the honored, embalmed body. Furthermore, the reviewers did not take into account that von Trier never intended to create an adaptation of Euripides' play in the first place. Viewers were advised through an inserted text prior to the film's opening scene that the film was made as homage to von Trier's great idol Carl Th. Dreyer. The indulgence in imagery is part of this celebration of one of the great masters of film art, and it is a continuation of the explorative take on the film as a medium for art that also characterized Dreyer's films.

To be fair there were two exceptions from the hostile reception in the dailies. The *eminence grise* of play critics, Jens Kistrup, defended von Trier's attempt to make *Medea* anew and he saw the film as daring and visually striking. Following the disapproving reception there were also other critics who defended the film as an independent work of art in its own right, and especially the attempt to drag the 'television theatre' out of its conservative and obsolete aesthetic norms.

Euripides' *Medea*

The myth about Jason and the Golden Fleece is part of a well established canon in Western culture. The myth tells the story of how Jason's father, King Aeson, lost his country, Iolcus, to his brother, Pelias. Jason grew up and returned to Iolcus to regain the throne. To prevent him from this endeavor Pelias puts him to an insurmountable test demanding of him the capture of the Golden Fleece guarded by the winged ram, Chrysomallus. In return for the Golden Fleece the King promises to hand over the right to the country to Jason. Jason goes to Colchis to search for the Golden Fleece. But as is the case in these matters things get complicated. The sorcerer Medea, who is the grandchild of the Sun and the daughter of King Aeëtes, falls in love with

Jason. Jason and Medea pledge eternal fidelity and she helps him through magic to obtain his goal. When discovered, they flee from Colchis with the Golden Fleece. They are nearly captured and Medea kills her little brother and throws him out of the boat in small pieces, delaying the followers who stop to pick up the pieces of the slain body. When they return to Iolcus, Medea tricks the daughters of King Aeson into killing their own father to rejuvenate him. Jason and Medea, therefore, flee again and they settle in Corinth where King Creon allows them to stay.

Euripides' play commences after these events and after Jason has married King Creon's daughter Glauce. At the centre of the play is the jealousy of Medea and the revenge she takes on Jason when she is expelled from Corinth by King Creon, who fears what pain she will cause him and his family due to her rage combined with her witchcraft. Euripides stresses a more psychological core than was usual in his times. Euripides was considered one of a new generation in Greek tragedy in that he emphasizes an understanding of human beings rather than the interests of Gods. Euripides was also progressive on the question on women's rights, which is obvious in the play *Medea* where discussions about the division of labor and the division on rights between the sexes are central issues.

In the opening of Euripides's *Medea* the nurse gives the background information to let the spectator into the plot of the story. She speaks about the Golden Fleece and the escape from Colchis. She laments on the events that have led Medea away from her native country to follow Jason, and she goes on to describe the sorrow and anguish of Medea due to Jason's treason:

> *Now all is hatred: love is sickness-stricken. For Jason, traitor to his babes and her, my mistress, weddeth with a child of kings, Daughter of Creon ruler of the land. And, slighted thus, Medea, hapless wife cries on the oaths, invokes that mightiest pledge of the right hand, and calls the Gods to witness what recompense from Jason she receives. (p.14-22)*[vi]

She finds Medea dangerous. She speaks about the outrage and what Medea is capable of against those who have betrayed her. The nurse exclaims: 'She loathes her babes, joys not beholding them. And what she may devise I dread to think, grim is her spirit, one that will not brook mishandling' (p.36-37).

The narrative proper begins with the entering of the pedagogue (or the children's guardian) and his announcement that the king of Corinth, Creon, will exile Medea and her sons from the country. The nurse warns that the children should be kept away from their devastated mother. She furthermore claims that she has observed that Medea has stared at the children in ways she does not like. She anticipates that the wrath of Medea might strike her loved ones as well as her enemies – that is first and foremost Jason but also the king and his daughter Glauce. Thereby she places the children as the center of our concern.

After the first scene, the play develops through seven scenes interrupted by the chorus of women inhabitants of Corinth. The women feel sorry for Medea and they side with her. They also try to persuade Medea to accept her position as a woman and to endure. The women of the play take the traditional conservative stance on the 'woman question'. They are challenged by Medea, who claims that she prefers to be a man and that women are only objects for men, whereas she wants to take control of her own life.

The second scene is a dialogue between King Creon and Medea where he tells her to leave the country or she will be executed. She plays the role of the submissive and weaker sex and she convinces Creon to allow her one day delay before her departure, explaining that she will not be able to do any harm with so short notice. The expelling of Medea from Corinth, nevertheless, forces her to take action and she develops a horrible scheme to cause as much pain as possible for Jason. Her plan has only one flaw: she has nowhere to go after her revenge is carried out. In the third scene, Jason pays a visit to Medea. He tries to convince her that he does not love Glauce but is only marrying her to secure his and Medea's children's safety and subsequent involvement in power. Jason's choice is entirely one of reason and for the benefit of them all. Medea is all but convinced.

In the succeeding scene Medea accidentally meets King Aegeus of Athens who promises that Medea will always be welcomed at his palace whatever happens. The two of them make a deal that Medea will help him out of his childlessness and in turn he will protect her. There is only one condition: Medea will have to reach Athens by herself:

> But thus it is – if to my land thou come, I will protect thee all I can: my right is this; but I forewarn thee of one thing – Not from this land to lead thee I consent; but, if thou reachest of thyself

> *mine halls, safe shalt thou bide; to none will I yield thee. But from this land thou must thyself escape; for even to strangers blameless will I be. (p.723-730)*

In the fifth scene, Medea pretends to be remorseful and apologizes for her behavior towards Jason when she disputed his reason for marrying Glauce. She asks Jason to take care of their two boys, who will be allowed to stay in Corinth. As a token for the children's and Medea's acceptance of Glauce's position, the boys will carry priceless presents to Glauce. The presents are part of Medea's scheme, and when Glauce takes on the golden crown and the weightless gown in scene six, she dies a painful death. Her father tries to rescue her and is struck by the poison as well. The subsequent scene seven is pivotal in the play. At the dramatic and psychological center of the play is Medea's struggle to murder her own children. After the death of Creon and Glauce she now has to kill the children to spare them a much more painful death from the hands of Corinthian soldiers: 'Friends, my resolve is taken, with all speed. To slay my children, and to flee this land, and not to linger and to yield my sons to death by other hands more merciless. They needs must die: and, since it needs must be, even I will give them death, who gave them life' (p.1236-1243). The play closes with a last meeting between Jason and Medea in the minutes after the Sun, Medea's grandfather, has sent her a chariot for her escape with the bodies of the boys, depriving Jason even of the chance to bury them.

von Trier's *Medea*

The core of Euripides' play is actually preserved in von Trier's adaptation. It is the same story about a woman in distress, Medea, who kills princess Glauce, King Creon and her sons to avenge her abandonment by her husband, Jason. The dialogues are also largely loyal to Euripides' 2000-year-old play. But the adaptation also contains estrangement effects in disparate spaces of sound and image, and a clearly perceptible visual style that features murky brownish monochrome images and vibrant contrasting colors in specific scenes, and multilayered images in others.

The background for the adaptation was a script for a film written in the mid 1960s by Carl Th. Dreyer and Preben Thomsen. The script was Dreyer's attempt to find the story behind the myth as he had done with great artistic success *The Passion of Joan of Arc* (1928). In that film Dreyer used the real documents from the trial against Joan of Arc, and he told the story from the point of view of historical accuracy. At the same time Dreyer also tried to display Joan from a psychological point of view – as a human being more than the myth created by her courageous deeds. Hence, we see her doubts, agony and angst as an inner conflict enhanced by the pressure from her wardens and tormentors. At the same time the film takes visual advantage of white walls and close-ups of Joan (Renée Falconetti) and creates a cinematic aesthetic of depthlessness within the picture frame.

In Euripides' *Medea*, Dreyer may have found an equal in the interest for psychological examination of beleaguered female characters. And if Euripides is considered the Greek tragedian that moved the tragedy towards human beings and in some respect a more realistic direction, Dreyer made an effort to make the film even more realistic due to his interest in psychological realism. He found the end of the story, where Medea is rescued via *deus ex machina* (the Sun's intervention by sending a chariot), unacceptable. The idea of Medea in the end leaving on a boat with King Aegeus is from Dreyer's original script (Schepelern 2000, pp.136-139). But it is a clear violation of the argument Aegeus put forward to Medea.

According to Lars von Trier, the film is not first and foremost an adaptation of Euripides' play and perhaps even not an adaptation of the script by Dreyer and Thomsen. An opening title preceding the film informs: 'This film is made from a script by Carl T. Dreyer and Preben Thomsen after Euripides's drama *Medea*. Carl T. Dreyer never realized his script. This is not an attempt to make a 'Dreyer' film, but with due reverence to the material a personal interpretation and homage to the master. Lars von Trier'. In this chapter I will take a closer look at what he might have meant by 'a personal interpretation'. First, I will take a closer look at the dramaturgy of the film.

Table 1: The narrative structure of *Medea*

Euripides' *Medea*	Lars von Trier's *Medea*
	I A Opening with Medea on the shore
	I B The deal with Aegeus. [4]
	I C Intertitle: "Medea" followed by background information on the mission of Argo. [1]
	II The wedding between Jason and Glauce. [Referred to by the nurse in 1.] (Intercut: Medea with her boys)
1. Opening: Background information about the Argonauts and the plea between Jason and Medea. Medea's mourning and anger. The support of her friends.	III Medea's monologue about women's rights and revenge. [1. and 6.] (Intercut: Jason awakens shortly when Medea says 'revenge')
2. King Creon exiles Medea giving her one day to leave. Medea develops a plan for revenge.	IV King Creon exiles Medea giving her one day to leave.
3. The quarrel between Jason and Medea.	V The quarrel between Jason and Medea.
4. The deal with Aegeus.	VI Aegeus passes by and confirms his agreement with Medea.
5. The scheme with Jason and the children.	VII Medea's scheme with Jason and the boys.
6. The painful death of Glauce and King Creon.	VIII The horse dies on the shore.
7. The killing of the boys, off stage.	IX The killing of the boys.
8. Medea departs on the chariot sent by her grandfather the Sun.	X Medea departs on King Aegeus' ship.

In its overall dramaturgy the adaptation follows the structure of the play. There are only a few deviations. In von Trier's film we actually see Medea killing her sons; Eurpides' version presents the killing off-stage. However, von Trier's depiction of the killing has no effect on the dramaturgy. The explicit depiction of the murder has of course an impact on the viewer in that it reinforces the emotive effect and it also makes Medea's sacrifice more evident, in that her grief is shown and not merely related through dialogue. Also the depiction of the wedding between Jason and Glauce is added to the narrative of the film in place of the announcement by the nurse. All the dialogue following the wedding is of course also added. The dialogue suggests that Jason's new wife, Glauce, is involved in the deportation of

Medea. Glauce refuses Jason a place in the wedding bed until Medea is out of the country. Although this addition emphasizes the sentiments of the women it does not influence the narrative and Glauce's jealousy is not hinted at anymore in the film.

Medea's deal with King Aegeus is split into two scenes (I B and VI in Table 1), which in fact is a violation of the logic inherent in Euripides' play in that Medea's hesitation in her vengeance is caused by the problem with her secured future refuge. One of the components in Medea's inner conflict is thus removed by placing the deal before the actual narrative. In the play Aegeus' accidentally meeting with Medea seems to happen in a very opportune moment and more to the necessity of the plot development than (realistically) motivated or explained within the framework of the play itself. Finally, the last meeting between Medea and Jason in which Jason realizes what is the outcome of Medea's outrage is omitted and replaced by images of an anguished and lonely Jason driven to madness. Beside these changes von Trier takes advantage of the possibility to make intercuts in scenes and crosscuts between scenes.

The only genuine addition to the narrative is the opening sequence, in which we see Medea lying on a shore and subsequently very slowly covered by the tide. She disappears interminably before she rises from the water, gasping for air. This added scene is very suggestive and at the same time rather opaque in meaning. It connects Medea with the element of water and suggests that she has certain powers that are of another world. The opening implies that Medea is superhuman, indicating to the viewer her relationship to a God. The opening also suggests that she is very willful and headstrong. But beside these common symbolic meanings the opening places the narrative in a certain space: that of cinematic imagery. I will return to this discussion below. A second part of the opening shows King Aegeus approaching on a ship drawn by his men in the shallow water of a tidal area. This suggestive and strong image is repeated later in the when we see men drawing a train in the same manner.

Into the Telefilm

The opening scene in von Trier's *Medea* shows her in an enigmatic montage of images. The film opens with a black screen and the sound of birds. The image fades in and we see Medea relaxed or dead. Her eyes are shut and she is completely innate. But then, she suddenly opens her mouth and takes a deep breath, apparently in pain or agony. The opening image is taken directly from above, making it impossible to obtain any sense of depth. It is not possible from the image to decide whether Medea is lying down or standing up against an uneven concrete wall. The monochrome image makes much visual information imperceptible or ambiguous and it is therefore impossible to tell what the background in the image consists of. After a little while it becomes clear that she actually is lying down on a shore. The camera slowly begins to spin as we hear strings on the soundtrack. The spinning speeds up and the recognizable image disappears and dissolves into an image of water running into the shore. Then there is a cut to Medea who clenches her right fist in the sand. The image dissolves to show water slowly washing up the shore, and then a quick dissolve to Medea who clenches her other fist. Then we see the water getting closer to the woman and it begins to overflow her. As the water gradually covers Medea's body, the camera is also being covered until it is under water. Then there is a dissolve to an image of a vast sea with a still surface. We wait and nothing happens until Medea suddenly rises up from the water and breathes heavily as if she has held her breath for a very long time. The sound has throughout been a mix of somber strings and bird cries.

This opening shows Medea in great pain. It is, though, a very puzzling opening with a narrative next to and outside the narrative proper, which begins with the arrival of King Aegeus in the second scene in the opening sequence. What does the opening scene mean by showing Medea lying on the sea shore? And why is she supposedly drowned or kept under water for too long for a human being to survive? The opening scene is perhaps more comprehensible when it is compared with other films by von Trier. Nearly all the works by von Trier have a split narrative in which the storytelling constitutes a specific layer in the film: a voice over as in most of his films; clearly distinctive different visual styles and intertitles as in *Breaking the Waves* (1996); or a depiction of the filming crew and simulated documentary interviews as in *The Idiots* (1998). The only film without this explicitly split narrative is *Medea*, where there is no clear indication of an overt mediator or narrator position. (Another possible exception is *Dancer in the Dark*, 2000.) There are, however a lot of indirect signs of another layer. These are only hinted at within the visual depiction. I will return to these features later.

The first part of the opening is outside the narrative and it must be seen as a transition passage from one realm to another. The transition works on three different levels. I here adopt the understanding of a text as consisting of discourse, diegesis and narration. The discourse is the material (words, images, sounds) available for the reader or spectator. The *diegesis* is the fictitious world the discourse refers to. All the action and the dialogues take place on the *diegetic* level. The third level is the act of narration and, hence, the level of communication where an addressee is implied. The only level that is present is the discourse. The two other levels are implied by the discourse.

The most immediate of the transitions takes place on the level of the diegesis; it is through the illusion of a self-sufficient universe that the spectator gains access to into the cinematic discourse. Medea is going through a phase from being a passive victim to becoming actively involved in the vengeance. Her suffering has to be dealt with and she is seeking strength for the action to come. That is also to say that she is attuning to the situation to become part of her own story. On this diegetic level she is also positioned as a superhuman in union with nature. The water is shown as her real element. The force of nature is anticipated to be set against the societal forces represented by King Creon and Jason.

On the discourse level, the character Medea is animated to be part of a story. She is lying, presumably dead, until someone or something breathes life into her. Is it an act of God or the creator of the story? Medea as a character is given life by something outside the story. As with most other characters from von Trier's films in the 1980s, she is a puppet in the hands of a director-puppeteer. It is therefore no surprise that she can be under water for a very long time. On this level, the opening suggests that the story is initiated by Medea's transition from an inanimate being to a character with a mission. She begins her own (fictitious) life after she reemerges from the ocean and speaks her first words following her second deep breath, suggesting that she is (re)born and baptized.

On a third level, this transition is positioned on an axis of communication between the film material and the spectator or reader. This is not to be understood as the bodily reader but as the structural implication of the discourse. Just as the telling of a story implies a storyteller whether this narrator is presented as a narrator or not, the story as an act of communication implies a reader position that is addressed. The transitional stage here is the spectator's acceptance to dispense of his or her disbelief and to go into the fiction, the diegetic world of *Medea*. To engage in fiction is to accept playing a game of suspension of disbelief. The opening scene is an aesthetic passage from the realm of reality to the realm of fiction; a guidance of the spectator from his or her own world into the fictitious world.

In a sense this tripartite function of the opening sequence equals the use of hypnosis in von Trier's early films. Von Trier's early films (those prior to *Breaking the Waves*, 1996) all work with hypnosis as a transitory passage both from reality to fiction and from one reality in the fiction (the diegesis proper) to the narration of the fiction in one way or another. In *The Element of Crime* (1984), the main narrative about the policeman Fisher and his investigations in Europe is narrated by Fisher himself during hypnosis. The opening scene shows an Egyptian hypnotist and Fisher, who after entering a trance narrates the story. The opening is a passage from one world of reality (the present of the film's time of narrative) into the diegesis within the film (the past), both for the characters and for the spectators, who are invited to follow the narration. A similar transitory passage is adopted in the end of von Trier's second film *Epidemic* (1987) in which two script writers present their finalized script to the state film consultant who will decide if they will receive funding for their film or not. The consultant does not appreciate that the film script is only twelve pages long and does not contain the story he had expected and thought they had agreed on. The script writers have invited a hypnotist and a 'medium' for a special presentation of the script. A girl will be hypnotized into the script. By this demonstration the script writers hope to show the script's viability. It turns out that the script indeed is very powerful in that the plague described in the script transgresses the script and infects all persons present at the presentation. They are all affected by the plague. This is an especially clear demonstration of an aesthetic idea present in von Trier's artistic universe. The transgressive plague is a metaphor for his cinematic poetic and it illustrates very well the idea of a passage between reality and fiction. The main characters do not notice that the script has had this disease-spreading effect throughout the film.

In *Europa* (1991), the voice of a hypnotist leads both the protagonist and the spectator into the film by hypnotizing 'us'. As the hypnotist (Max von Sydow's voice) says, you go deeper and deeper 'and on the count of ten you are in Europa'. The hypnotist leads the protagonist through different actions in the film until in the end he hypnotizes him for one last time: 'and on the count of ten you are dead' – and we the spectators now leave the fiction and are lead through a passage back to our own reality. The main character, though, has ceased to exist in that the fiction has ended. In *The Kingdom* (1994) the introductory sequence is also a hypnotic voice over. A deep, calm male voice slowly gives information on the ground under the Kingdom and the spectator is visually urged to go deeper and deeper – as in *Europa* – deeper into the (collective) subconscious and to let go of conscious control. This should not necessarily be understood in a psychoanalytical way, meaning going deeper into the hidden repressions of childhood drives and traumas. The hypnosis is better understood as an aesthetic device for suspending of everyday understandings to accept the fiction world or the realm of art. The films by von Trier form alternative worlds to the present society. This idea sounds like Romanticism but it is without the metaphysics that point to some transcendental being or primordial existence.

The passage between the realms of reality and that of fiction is a particular marker of the mediator of the film as fiction. All of von Trier's films are obviously staged and clearly 'told' in ways in which the telling and depiction become perceptible and evident. By different devices the implied narrator becomes visible both as the one who relates a story of fiction but also as the one who makes up this story. In a narratological sense there is a difference between the presentation of a story of fiction and the invention of the story, as Seymour Chatman has shown in *Coming to Terms* (1990):

> *[For] films as for novels, we would do well to distinguish between a* presenter *of the story, the narrator (who is a component of the discourse), and the* inventor *of both the story and the discourse (including the narrator): that is, the implied author – not as the original cause, the original biographical person, but rather as the principle within the text to which we assign the inventional tasks. (1990, p.133)*

The three functions of the opening scene I have called attention to point towards these levels of narration, the presenter and the inventor.

Applied to a general understanding of cinematic narration, the notion of a cinematic narrator (mediator) is disputed. The visual depiction is habitually seen as giving direct access to the fictional world, the diegesis. In his influential book *Narration in the Fiction Film* (1985), David Bordwell rejects the idea of cinematic mediation as something similar to literary fiction. The written text indicates a writer/narrator as an implied author.

The implied author has since Wayne Booth's *The Rhetoric of Fiction* (1961) been understood as a simulated position within the text that shapes internal values due to verbal choices and point of views of the depiction, and this position is not to be misunderstood as representing the author as an ethical being – at least not in any simple manner. The text itself (*syuzhet*, plot) is a depiction of what has happened (*fabula*, story) for some characters and the transference from story to plot is an interpretation that partly shapes the story world by the ways in which it is related.

Contrary to the literary representation through a simulated mind, the spectator of a film, goes the argument, actually sees what happens and there is no interpretative level as in written fiction, where different words and the whole tonality of the work is understood to have an impact on the meaning. 'No trait we could assign to an implied author of a film could not more simply be ascribed to the narration itself: it sometimes suppresses information, it often restricts our knowledge, it generates curiosity, it creates a tone, and so on. To give every film a narrator or implied author is to indulge in an anthropomorphic fiction', says Bordwell (1985, p.62). A girl described as thin, skinny or slim evokes different pictures in the mind of the reader. But if a girl is shown for the spectator she appears as she is without the verbal interpretation of her shape. The girl is hence presented and not *re-presented* in a supplementary way, as in verbal language.

The language sign is arbitrary and calls for a code for transmittance to a mental idea. Contrarily, the cinematic sign, it is further claimed, is not a sign proper in that it directly shows what is meant, and no translation is necessary. The verbal language implies a *concept* whereas the visual, cinematic depiction constitutes a *percept*. This understanding developed by George Bluestone is advanced by Brian McFarlane (1996) when he describes the differences between the literary and the cinematic sign systems: '[T]he verbal sign, with its low iconicity and high symbolic function, works *conceptually*, whereas the cinematic sign, with its high iconicity and uncertain symbolic function, works directly, sensuously, *perceptually*' (p.26).

It is difficult to accept that there is less indulgence in 'anthropomorphic fiction,' in Bordwell's description, of the acts of the narration in opposition to the interpretative choices of an implied author or narrator. What is at stake is the ascribing of certain intentional acts which influence the depiction, making it less a window to the narrative actions than a rendering, a (told) representation of these. It seems that Bordwell agrees in this understanding of the matter when he claims, 'A film's *fabula* is never materially present on the screen or soundtrack' (1985, p.49). The evident consequence of the idea that there is no direct access to the *fabula* (story world) is that the filmic discourse in all its details is a representation, and this representation is doing something with the information it passes to the spectator. It does not matter whether this interpretation is ascribed to 'the narration' or 'a narrator'; the one is no more and no less anthropomorphized than the other and they are both interpreted as implied by the cinematic discourse. Bordwell, however, maintains that it is important to ascribe the representation to the narration because it underlines the active role of the spectator in making meaning out of the cues in the text. But as Chatman (1990) also points out in his sympathetic critique of Bordwell, there is a textual level of the narrative too, and the interpretations of spectators are not just the result of an abstract cueing: 'In my view, it is not that the viewer constructs but that she *reconstructs* the film's narrative (along with other features) from the set of cues encoded in the film' (1990, p.127). The cues interpreted are themselves inscribed in a narrative structure as the syntagmatic ordering system of the text. By neglecting the textual level – the discourse – Bordwell abandons textual analyses altogether.

The advantage of using the term 'narrator' is that it allows for further distinctions, as for example Gerard Genette's (1980) tripartite model, where he makes distinctions between discourse (the text be it written or visual), *story*, and narrating. He proposes to 'use the word *story* for the signified or narrative content ... the word *narrative* for the signifier, statement, discourse or narrative text itself, and to use the word *narrating* for the producing narrative action and, by extension, the whole of the real or fictional situation in which that action takes place' (p.27). The only manifest level is the narrative discourse. Story and the activity of narrating are in a sense not existent but interpretations of the discourse's implications as I have stated above.

In my reading the distinction between the different levels of the text is a way to understand the particular way in which the narrative about Medea is told. To understand von Trier's adaptation of Euripides' play it is essential to account for the layers within the images and within the discourse as a whole. In *Medea* there is an abundance of indirect signs indicating the presence of a presenter and an inventor as is shown above.

In the second scene in the opening sequence there is another example of the film's deviations from conventional cinematic narratives. Medea talks with King Aegeus and their dialogue is primarily *sotto voce* despite the visual fact that they are placed far apart from each other. The voices are clearly audible for the spectator but have to be impossible to hear for the characters if the visual information accurately depicts their spatial arrangement. Nevertheless, the two characters clearly respond to each other. The stage-whispered dialogue is by no means realistically motivated, but rather stylistically motivated. The disparity between sound and images indicates the presence of a sovereign narrator who exclusively controls the distribution of information to the reader; information created independently of a story that already has taken place. At the very least the discourse is not just delivering information from a story world but is calling attention to the discourse itself and the creative process of narrating.

The discourse in von Trier's *Medea* is doubled and redoubled by making use of shadows, transparent screens, frames within frames, mirrors in troubled water, unrealistic colors, and so on and so forth. Also the texture of the images is clearly manipulated and thereby insistent as a visual marker of the presence of the medium and the artificiality of the narrative. The monochrome and obscured image was obtained by the special process of recordings and transference of the material. *Medea* was filmed on video and afterward the video recordings were transferred to film stock. The film was then transferred to another video format. By these transferences much visual information was lost. The process of transferences taken together with insufficient lightning during the recordings obscured the images. This process, however, has also given the images a very tactile quality. The result is that the discourse is very adamant. By different features in the discourse *Medea* creates a space of enunciation, as I have tried to show above.[vii]

Out of the Telefilm

In von Trier's *Medea* most of the changes from Euripides and Dreyer are to be found in the use of the visual. Peter Schepelern (2000) notes that 'first and foremost Trier has chosen to use the television media…to display a visual experiment related to the avant-garde film' (pp.139-140). The made-for-television film looks neither like a film nor like television nor video. The 'film' creates its own cinematic style as a monstrosity. It is an examination of the visual and narratological options in different media combined in the film.

It is clear that the visual style and the way in which the film is narrated created the uproar by critics and viewers when the film was broadcast. The reaction was caused by the unusual realization of something that is only a script by Euripides. The history of dramatic adaptations of *Medea* has created a specific tradition for realizations. All theatrical realizations, however, are adaptations and, hence, interpretations. The idea of a virgin text – or a correct adaptation – is untenable. The tradition was challenged by von Trier's adaptation of the classical text. Von Trier's adaptation relocated the text and this re-contextualization made the play appear as something very different from the conventional adaptations. The effect was that the realization in itself became palpable which was seen as obscuring the original.

To some extent the critics were right. The film *Medea* is not particularly interested in celebrating a dead author and a dead text. Therefore, it is not trying to be true to the conceptions of what the eternal, intrinsic values of Euripides' text are. However, the film revivifies some ideas that are also detectable in Euripides' script and its narrative. One of the ingredients is the suffering of a woman and her reactions to this suffering. The motive of a suffering woman who actually is both special and strong is as central to Dreyer and von Trier as it was to Euripides. Dreyer could make use of Euripides' play to go more thoroughly into an investigation of the psychology of the woman. Von Trier could make use of Euripides' play and Dreyer's script to go into the cinematic potentials of the suffering woman combined with an examination of the aesthetic potentials of the medium of television as something more than a neutral transmitter of information. From this point of view the realization was very successful.

Von Trier has used his *Medea* to go deeper and deeper into the 'woman in distress' motif he also later was to explore in the 'Golden Heart Trilogy': *Breaking the Waves*, *The Idiots*, and *Dancer in the Dark*. Bess, Karen and Selma (protagonists of the films) are true sisters of Medea – as they are of Joan of Arc. When Euripides adapted the myth of the Golden Fleece, he transformed its content according to what he felt or sensed was important in his own times. He was widely criticized for his neglect of the Gods and the way he changed the role of the chorus. But he perhaps understood that eternal ethical and artistic values have to be changed for a story to live on. By adapting the narrative from Euripides' play and using it for an artistic remediation, von Trier aligns himself with Euripides both artistically and ethically.

REFERENCES
Booth, W. (1961) *The Rhetoric of Fiction*. Chicago: Chicago University Press.
Bordwell, D. (1985) *Narration in the Fiction Film*. London: Methuen.
Christensen, Ove & Claus Falkenstrøm (ed.) (2004) *Space Oddity. Det filmiske rum i von Triers Medea* [Space Oddity. The Cinematic Space in von Trier's *Medea*]: *På kant med værket* [On the Edge of the Work of Art]. Copenhagen.
Chatman, S. (1990) *Coming to Terms: The Rhetoric of Narrative in Fiction and Film*. Ithaca, NY: Cornell University Press.
Crimp, D. (1983) 'On the Museum's Ruins' in H. Foster (ed.) *The Anti-Aesthetic: Essays on Postmodern Culture*, pp.43-56. New York: New Press.
Euripides (1971-1978) 'Medea', in *Euripides IV*. Cambridge, MA: Harvard University Press.
Genette, G. (1980) *Narrative Discourse: An Essay in Method* (J.E. Lewin, trans.). Ithaca, NY: Cornell University Press.
Genette, G. (1987) *Narrative Discourse Revisited* (J.E. Lewin, trans.). Ithaca, NY: Cornell University Press.
McFarlane, B. (1996) *Novel to Film: An Introduction to the Theory of Adaptation*. Oxford: Clarendon Press.
Schepelern, P. (2000) *Lars von Triers Film. Tvang og Befrielse*. Copenhagen: Rosinante.

FILMS REFERENCED
von Trier, L. (dir.) (1984) *The Element of Crime*. Denmark: Janus Films.
von Trier, L. (dir.) (1987) *Epidemic*. Denmark: Element Film.
von Trier, L. (dir.) (1988) *Medea*. Denmark: Danish Broadcasting Corporation.
von Trier, L. (dir.) (1991) *Europa*. Denmark: Nordic Film/TV Association.
von Trier, L. (dir.) (1996) *Breaking the Waves*. Denmark: Zentropa.
von Trier, L. (dir.) (2000) *Dancer in the Dark*. Denmark: Fine Line Features
von Trier, L. (dir.) & M. Arnfred (ass. dir.) (1994) *The Kingdom*. Denmark: October Films.

NOTES
[ii] In 1988 Danish Broadcasting Corporation was the only Danish broadcasting television channel. It is therefore likely that the majority of the population more or less intensively saw the film. Later in 1988 the status of monopoly was replaced by a two-channel structure and a number of commercial satellite channels also broke into the market.
[iii] The reviews of Lars von Trier's *Medea* are treated in Me Lund: 'Receptionen af tv-filmen *Medea*' [The reception of the television film *Medea*] in a special issue on von Trier: *Sekvens. Filmvidenskabelig årbog* 1991 pp.125-140.
[iv] Ibid.p.128
[v] Ibid.p.130
[vi] All references to the lines in the play are put in parenthesis. I have changed the capital letter beginning new lines when in conflict with the grammar.
[vii] I have more extensively analyzed the different cinematic spaces and the structure of enunciation in *Medea* in the chapter: "Space Oddity. Det filmiske rum i von Triers *Medea*" [Space Oddity. The Cinematic Space in von Trier's *Medea*], Ove Christensen and Claus Falkenstrøm (ed.): *På kant med værket* [On the Edge of the Work of Art], Copenhagen 2004, pp.184-223.

Found in Translation
Domestic-Universal Strategy in Adapting *Babette's Feast*

Gunhild Agger

A Dual Orientation

The film, *Babette's Feast*, was based on a tale by Karen Blixen (Isak Dinesen) and directed by Gabriel Axel. Dinesen and Axel represent a Danish as well as an international cultural horizon.

Dinesen's tales combined mythical elements with an understanding of both national and international traditions, and from the very start she practised a dual language strategy as regards publishing. Gabriel Axel worked alternatively in Denmark and France as an actor and a director of films and television drama. It is only a logical consequence of both Dinesen's and Axel's mixed cultural heritage that *Babette's Feast* offers a dual orientation. In the following, I will discuss how this dual orientation works in the tale and in the film, introducing the idea of a domestic-universal combination strategy. As I consider the fidelity of transformation a key term in this adaptation, it is necessary to start with the beginning – the author and the tale – before analyzing the film. Translations are mine except otherwise indicated.

The Author

Karen Blixen (1885-1962) was a sophisticated writer with an intellectual as well as a certain popular appeal. Karen Blixen loved a masquerade. The pseudonyms that she applied offer a privileged entrance to major themes in her oeuvre. Consequently, I shall briefly reflect on them. Her first tale was published in 1907 under the name Osceola (an Indian chieftain fighting for independence), and in *The Angelic Avengers* from 1944 'Pierre Andrézel' figured as the author. Her prevalent nom de plume in the USA and England was Isak Dinesen. Dinesen was her maiden name. The choice of her father's surname can be seen as an allegiance to his authorship and the values it defended.[viii] Choosing Isak as a first name may hint at several issues. Isak is a man's name. The literature from the 19th century exhibits other examples of women writers making use of a male pseudonym, e.g. George Eliot in England and George Sand in France. Judith Thurman, one of Isak Dinesen's most thorough biographers, has the following comment: 'If "Isak" Dinesen took a man's name, it was at least partly to get a man's freedom' (1986, p.300). No doubt, Karen Blixen welcomed the opportunity to acquire a masculine role. Besides, the name Isak is loaded with biblical connotations. God explicitly asked Abraham to call his late born son Isak, and the name means 'he laughs' (*First Book of Moses*, chapter 17, verse 19). Sara laughed, too, when she heard that she was to become a mother in her old age. Isak is not only a man, but also a double – a victim and a ruler. Isak was the son of Abraham, and one of the most impressive tales in the *First Book of Moses* treats the sacrifice of Isak. Later, Isak became one of the patriarchs. Accordingly, the choice of pseudonym for Blixen's English editions contains elements of her essential themes of view: the value of understanding that we are all performers; the importance of tales and myth in human life; the similarity between God and the artist; and last but not least, the divine irony.

The début of Karen Blixen took place in 1934 when *Seven Gothic Tales* appeared in the USA. *Seven Gothic Tales* conveys the reflections of a disappearing aristocratic culture in a way that transcends the affiliation to this very culture. Disguised in gothic vaults and veils the basic questions persist: What is the meaning of all the masquerades? Which kind of reality is hidden behind the roles performed? How is the meaning conveyed by the artists?

The reception was favourable by both critics and audience. The Book-of-the-Month Club as its February selection chose *Seven Gothic Tales* even before the book appeared. The identity of the author was revealed in *The New York Herald Tribune* April 23, 1934. The American success inspired an English edition in September. Amongst English critics, opinions were divided. In *The Evening Standard* Sep. 6, 1934 Howard Spring called Dinesen 'a Danish Genius' (Andersen and Lasson 1980, p.116), but in *The Observer* Sep. 9, Gerard Gould labelled her style 'pompous' (Andersen and Lasson 1980, p.121). Several reviewers drew attention to the fact that the tales were written and published in a foreign language. In 1935 the tales were translated into Danish by the author. According to the introduction to the Danish edition, Blixen originally had an international audience in mind for the book:

> *When, for my own amusement, I wrote this book in English I didn't think it would have any interest for Danish readers. Now it has been its destiny to be translated into other languages, and it was therefore natural that it should also be published in my own country. [...] A great deal of* Seven Gothic Tales *was thought out and some of it written in Africa, and the places in my book which touch on Denmark must be taken as a Danish emigrant's fantasies on Danish themes, rather than as some attempt to give a picture of reality. (Thurman 1986, p.313)*

In Denmark as in England, critics were divided. Besides, reactions to the personality and destiny of Karen Blixen tended to colour their judgment. As a genre the gothic tale was unusual in Denmark during this period; realism and a social commitment prevailed. Most reviewers had an eye for the aesthetics of narration and expressed admiration of the author's unusual talent. A few quotations can support this idea. In *Politiken*, Tom Kristensen, the poet and critic, called the book 'brilliant' (Andersen and Lasson 1980, p.213). In *Dagens Nyheder* Hans Brix, the leading critic, wrote, 'It abounds in female shapeliness and male elegance as a Hollywood of literature. [...] It is beyond morals. And only preoccupied by the splendour of life. In its attitude to existence it is arrogantly aristocratic' (Andersen and Lasson 1980, p.212). Other critics could not acknowledge the relevance of this odd world from yesterday, this declared anti-modernism in 1935, as in the famous case of Frederik Schyberg. His headline in *Berlingske Tidende* read, 'A piece of dazzling, artistic imitation by a clever, but affected authoress' (Andersen and Lasson 1980, p.225).

The ambivalence in the Danish and English reviews may be due to the fact that Karen Blixen declined the modern world and preferred the past, usually the 18th and 19th centuries, as her choice of time. Accordingly, her social world is a world of yesterday. The aristocracy, its manners, values and way of looking at the world – as well as its servants – play an important part. So does the old peasantry. Other characters are clergymen, students and merchants. Seen from a modern and a social point of view, the over-representation of nobility, servants and peasantry can be interpreted as a limit to the relevance of her tales. Though the aristocratic world of Karen Blixen may have attracted readers at home and abroad, it is more likely that readers in the first place were (and are) attracted to the themes, the plots and the art of narration. According to an introduction by Karen Blixen recorded after her visit to the USA in 1959, she considered herself a 'storyteller' in the tradition of Homer, the Bible and the sagas (With 1964, p.213). Like her predecessors, her tales are occupied with universal questions – the meaning of life, love, art and fate, themes that she highlights again and again from various perspectives. These often include references to national traditions and culture. I would like to suggest the term *domestic-universal combination strategy* as an appropriate concept for Karen Blixen's dual orientation.

In a 1956 interview with *The Paris Review*, Karen Blixen said that the American audience was her first and most faithful (Andersen and Lasson 1980, p.64). Robert Langbaum notes that 'if the Danes discovered her a year later than we did and had more reservations about her, they also took her from the beginning more seriously than we did' (1964, p.3). Langbaum contributed to the understanding of her authorship, especially by showing how the special quality of combining and reconciling opposites, which Karen Blixen acquired in Africa, kept sustaining themes and plots (1964, p.6). Africa provided her with the alien eye, the physical and spiritual distance that she needed for her unusual literary enterprise. Karen Blixen retained her dual language strategy as regards publishing. Her books were published either simultaneously, or very closely, in the USA or England and Denmark (Table 2).

For several years, Karen Blixen seemed to have two main audiences[x] The American audience had no reservations to those elements in the authorship that fitted into popular culture and made the selections of book-of-the-month possible. The audience in Denmark and England seemed as preoccupied with the narrative charms as the American audience. But in Denmark the question of taking Karen Blixen seriously (Langbaum 1964), of her relationship to the national cultural heritage, and of fitting 'the Baroness' into a contemporary Danish context held a stronger position in public debate. In a Danish context the elementary entertaining dimensions were underestimated (Agger 1988).

Table 2: List of Main Publications in Danish and English[ix]

Year	In Danish (Karen Blixen)	In English (Isak Dinesen)
1934		*Seven Gothic Tales* (Book of the Month), New York. London
1935	*Syv Fantastiske Fortællinger* (Isak Dinesen)	
1937	*Den Afrikanske Farm*	*Out of Africa*, London
1938		*Out of Africa* (Book of the Month), New York
1942	*Vinter-Eventyr*	*Winter's Tales* (Book of the Month), New York. London
1944	*Gengældelsens Veje* (Pierre Andrézel)	
1946		*The Angelic Avengers*, London (Pierre Andrézel)
1947		*The Angelic Avengers* (Book of the Month), New York (Pierre Andrézel)
1957	*Sidste Fortællinger*	*Last Tales*, New York. London
1958	*Skæbne-Anekdoter*	*Anecdotes of Destiny*, New York. London
1960	*Skygger paa Græsset*	
1961		*Shadows on the Grass*, New York. London
1963	*Ehrengard*	*Ehrengard*, New York. London
1965	*Essays*	
1975	*Efterladte Fortællinger*	
1977		*Entertainments and Posthumous Tales*, Chicago
1978	*Breve fra Afrika: 1914-1931*	
1979		*Daguerreotypes and Other Essays*, Chicago
1981		*Letters from Africa: 1914-1931*, London

Babette's Feast – the Tale

Babette's Feast is one of the tales by Karen Blixen that was written in English and originally published in *Ladies' Home Journal*, June 1950. In November 1950, Bodil Ipsen, the popular Danish actress, read a translation of *Babette's Feast* aloud on Radio Denmark. In 1952 it appeared in a book edition at 'Fremads Folkebibliotek'. Karen Blixen won the booksellers' prize The Golden Laurels for *Babette's Feast*, which proves the popularity this tale enjoyed. In 1958 she included *Babette's Feast* in her collection *Anecdotes of Destiny*.

Babette's Feast is composed of 12 small chapters with headings in a classical, transparent style, carefully told. The author's voice is full of authority. It takes care of structuring the time passing, selecting the peak episodes in a span of time encompassing 1785 as the year of the Dean's birth and 1950 as the time of narration as its extreme ends. The aspect of *time* is stressed by the author's voice, taking 'sixty-five years ago' (p. 23) as its point of departure.[xi] Consequently, I shall characterise the tale's relationship to time in the following.

In the first chapter, each sentence hides a drama that will be revealed during the rest of the tale. The main conflict between the concept of earthly love (as an illusion) and the spirituality of the new Jerusalem (as true reality) is established. The next two chapters are parallels, following the lovers of the Dean's two daughters: Lorens Loewenhielm who woos Martine in 1854, and Achilles Papin who woos Philippa in 1855. Both daughters are confronted with the demands of earthly love. The feelings evoked in the virgins are natural, but their upbringing has been so radical that is has deprived them of a language to be able to understand their own emotions: 'They lacked the words with which to discuss him' (p. 32). Both lovers have a vision. In Loewenhielm's case of a 'higher and purer life' (p. 26) and in Papin's case of a life dedicated to art – and dining at the Café Anglais in Paris (p. 31). The Dean doesn't have to reject the wooers. His daughters are brought up in a way that gives them little choice. The language in which the Dean expresses himself is the elevated biblical language of allegory. 'Mercy and Truth, dear Brethren, have met together', said the Dean, and 'Righteousness and Bliss have kissed one another' (p. 26). When Dean says, 'And God's paths run across the rivers, my child' (p. 31), the ever-present pressure on the daughters is stated. However, as the tale develops, it demonstrates that a broader understanding of the words of the scripture is possible.

Destiny has its own ways. The confrontation with the material world and the senses can be condensed to a few months, but the men so abruptly disappearing from the daughters' lives have their unexpected return. After a leap of time, in 1871,[xii] Babette arrives from Paris as a special envoy from Papin. In the character of Babette, material and artistic qualities are united. In his letter of introduction, Papin has printed the first two bars of the duet between Don Giovanni and Zerlina, as a sign of this – the duet that ended with the solemn kiss and Papin's departure. He states, 'Babette can cook' (p. 34).[xiii] As a result of Babette's arrival, the material daily life of the two sisters and of the poor maintained by their charity is transformed: the costs are reduced and the quality improved.

Whereas the chapters 1-5 are extended in time, the chapters 6-12 concentrate on one event. The pivotal point is the Dean's 100th anniversary – the preparations and expectations for it and the performance of Babette's masterpiece, the French dinner, on December 15. Thus Chapter 7 begins, 'In November' (p. 44), and Chapter 8 narrows the focus: 'On Sunday morning it began to snow'.[xiv] The dinner is the peak of the tale, the point to which all threads lead, only followed by the dénouement in Chapter 12. The title *Babette's Feast* underlines this as does the composition and the time span occupied by the dinner. The voice of the author explicitly states that there will be twelve guests for the dinner, thus discreetly comparing its significance to the last supper (Langbaum 1964, p.52) and the role of Babette to that of Jesus. Explicitly, the guests relate to the wedding of Cana (p. 55).

The dinner is a meeting place between former and present aspects of characters and ideas. Lorens Loewenhielm is not only confronted with Martine, but also with himself as he was 30 years ago, asking himself whether he made the right choices. The congregation is not only confronted with the conflict between the duty of forgiveness and the inclination of pettiness, but also with the contrast between the spiritual and the material world. And Lorens Loewenhielm, Martine and Philippa are confronted with their past choices. For the first time for 14 years, Babette has the opportunity of performing cooking as an art, contrasting her small daily miracles with the split cod and the ale-and-bread soup. Also Babette is confronted with her past, with her capability and ambition as an artist – and with her old audience, represented by the shadow of General Gallifet, who killed her husband and her son, and by Lorens Loewenhielm, who plays the role of the only audience educated to worship the artist. Accordingly, the understanding of Babette's brilliance is formulated by general Loewenhielm quoting the former colonel Gallifet: 'This woman is now turning a dinner at the Café Anglais into a kind of love affair – into a love affair of the noble and romantic category in which one no longer distinguishes between bodily and spiritual appetite or satiety!' (p. 58).

The quotation underlines the spirit in which the confrontations clash and in which the French dinner is consumed. A transformation takes place as it should at a communion table, changing secular time to the time of Jerusalem, 'one hour of the millennium' (p. 62), rejecting the dilemmas of both the congregation, Loewenhielm and the two sisters – thanks to the art of Babette, and behind her, Papin, the opera singer. The irony of the reunion of opposites is highlighted in Loewenhielm's speech. In his interpretation of the idea of mercy – that we get both what we have chosen and what we have refused – he has to reconsider his understanding as a young man. Then he argued, 'in this world there are things which are impossible!' (p. 27). Now 'Anything is possible' and Martine agrees (p. 62). Seen in this light, the quotation from the old Dean acquires a new meaning: 'For mercy and truth have met together, and righteousness and bliss have kissed one another!' (p. 60-62). The contrasts between past and present, choice and consequences, material and spiritual existence, are suspended.

The uneducated audience feels the miracle, but does not understand it. In ignorance they have denied themselves the opportunity to speak about what they eat and drink. This is underlined by Philippa's use of the epithet 'nice' about the dinner (p. 64). Loewenhielm feels and worships the miracle, but must make use of the elevated, biblical language, foreign to his real feelings, to convey it. The irony is that Babette, the cause of all this, is purely forgotten, a fact which corresponds to the genre, the anecdote of destiny. But according to Babette, one should not pity her, as she has had the pleasure of doing her utmost, which is the purpose of being for a great artist.

On a larger scale, the irony also concerns the concept of time in the tale. The effect of the author's disposition could be subsumed under the concept of relativity. Time passes; generations pass, but certain events and moments are as valuable as a whole lifetime. This is emphasized by the last passages of cosmic visions of snow and subsequently the stars: the singularity of artistic performance should be held in esteem. The place and setting are developed within the same frame of understanding: The humble cluster of houses situated at the periphery of culture, language, music etc., the pious congregation and the small community at the border of nothingness, neighbour to cosmos. The contrast to the educated audience in the big cities could not be more accentuated.

Summing up, the main themes of the tale are 1. *The irony of fate*: nothing turns out as expected. Threads from the past manifest themselves in the present. 2. *The ability of the artist to transform the world* – and the cry for possibilities to exert the utmost. Which is the precondition of the plot – and generally, the tales of Karen Blixen. 3. *Identity*. Does it change over time? This question is especially attached to Babette, and her dominant role in the tale can be ascribed to this.[xv] A tension in the plot evolves around her identity. Our acquaintance with her begins in the title where she figures as a mere name. During the first three chapters this name remains a riddle. In Papin's letter she is introduced as a) Mme. Babette Hersant, b) pétroleuse, and c) chef de cuisine. The brothers and sisters in the congregation recognize her as a dark Martha, but to Martine and Philippa she is also a Pythia (transmitter of the Oracles at Delphi). In a nightmare Martine sees her as a witch, preparing a Sabbath, and the idea of the pétroleuse, preparing the fall of society, keeps popping up. Lorens Loewenhielm at last can reveal her true identity as chef in the Café Anglais. And according to Babette herself – supported by the author's voice – her identity is that of a great artist, who by a supreme effort produces a work of art, which creates a marvellous effect although the main part of the audience is unable to appreciate it.

Adaptations of Karen Blixen's Works

Karen Blixen was not a cinematic kind of person herself. She was educated at the Royal Academy of Fine Arts and often referred to paintings in her tales. She recognized the artistic value of photography. During the 1950s, she made use of radio and television as means of communicating her opinions and her tales (Schepelern 1995, pp.15-16). But the urge to make adaptations of her works cannot be found in her own dispositions. Nevertheless, her works represented a challenge to filmmakers. *Babette's Feast* was not the first tale by Blixen to be adapted as a film.

Considering the predominant American attitude to Karen Blixen, it is only natural that American cinema contributed with two major adaptations. In 1968 Orson Welles directed *L'histoire immortelle* (*The Immortal Story*).

As with *Babette's Feast*, *The Immortal Story* is included in *Anecdotes of Destiny*. Orson Welles himself figured as dominant Mr. Clay, and Jeanne Moreau played the part of the young woman. The production was French. The adaptation represents a classic, exploring the power game between the sexes and the relationship between man and God in the art of creation and control.

The American film *Out of Africa* from 1985 is based on Blixen's autobiographical fiction *Out of Africa* 1937 and Judith Thurman's biography of Isak Dinesen, *The Life of Karen Blixen*, a book that attracted critical attention and won the American Book Award for Biography in 1983. Meryl Streep and Robert Redford added star quality to the performance. Sidney Pollack, the director, received an Academy Award for this film. With its tendency of mainstreaming *Out of Africa* and the biographical material, it made up an exhilarating but also a glamorous interpretation. No doubt, *Out of Africa* was a major source of inspiration for Danish directors. It represented a challenge to the Danish understanding that Karen Blixen's authorship had little relationship to popular culture.

In Denmark, television was predominant in adaptations. The Department of Television Drama adapted *Revenge of Truth* in 1961, directed by Erling Schroeder, and *Converse at Night in Copenhagen* in 1970, directed by Kasper Rostrup. In 1987 *Sorrow-acre* from *Winter's Tales*, directed by Morten Henriksen appeared, and in 1988 Kristoffer Nyholm contributed with *The Ring*. In 1982 *Ehrengard* was adapted in an Italian version for television. Gabriel Axel's film *Babette's Feast* from 1987 is singular.[xvi] Opposing the mainstreaming strategy in *Out of Africa*, it represented a cinematic attempt to mediate between cultures. This was recognized internationally in 1988 when *Babette's Feast* won the Academy Award in the category 'best foreign film'. Born in a French-Danish-Swedish pot, *Babette's Feast* managed to avoid the Euro-pudding-trap and to successfully apply a strategy for appealing to both national and international audiences.

Gabriel Axel

Gabriel Axel, the director, also wrote the script for *Babette's Feast*. Born in 1918, Axel had ample experience. Originally, he was educated as an actor. As such he worked both in Denmark and in France. From the very beginning in 1951, he became a director in the Danish Department of Television Drama. With fifty productions in eighteen years, he established himself as one of the most professional directors of Television Drama during this period. For French television he made *La Ronde de Nuit* (*The Night Watch*) in 1977, for which he was awarded the Balzac prize.

In 1955 he started his career as a feature film director. His first film was a socialist realistic production called *Nothing but Trouble*. Quickly, other genres appeared: the folk comedy (*Golden Mountains* 1958), the erotic comedy (*Crazy Paradise* 1962), and especially the heritage film (two films on the basis of Saxo: *Gesta Danorum – The Red Mantle* 1967: the legend of Hagbard and Signe; *The Prince of Jutland* 1994: the legend of prince Amled (Hamlet). Axel was open to various genres and apparently easily switched among cultures. *Babette's Feast* 1987 represented his comeback in Danish film after ten years of successful television drama productions in France.

Despite this dual orientation, Axel's attitude to the question of European identity and collaboration is not purely positive. From his point of view, such a thing as a European film is non-existent: 'In my mind a European film is a Danish film in Denmark, a French film in France, and so on. If we all nurture those differences, it will become a lot more exciting to listen to each other' (Hjort and Bondebjerg 2001, p.40). And he continues, 'If we want to be international we first and foremost have to be national. What the world needs is films that tell us something about how people live in Denmark, Sweden, France, Germany and so on' (p.40). To Axel, it would be much easier if co-production primarily was financial.

What Axel opposes here is the tendency to eliminate national characteristics in favour of the phenomenon that in Europe has been labelled a 'Europudding' – international films without an identity. It is a common trait in most of the Danish directors interviewed by Hjort and Bondebjerg that they strongly oppose this lack of identity, which can be the consequence of increased international cooperation.

Cross-filming and Other Combination Strategies

No doubt, Axel has benefited from the two cinematic cultures, which have made the consciousness of *cross-filming* self-evident for him. Perhaps so self-evident that he does not notice it himself.

Hjort identifies various concepts, which may be useful to define strategies for directors from minor film cultures (Hjort 1996, Agger 2001). Certain elements in a national film – and indeed certain films – can be considered *opaque*. Targeting a national culture, they are not translatable to an international audience without comments. For example, *The Gyldenkål Family* 1975, directed by Axel, related to the popular Olsen-gang films in ways which would only be appreciated by an audience familiar with the cast and style of traditional Danish folk comedy. Other elements – and other films – can be considered *translatable*. Although they may be culturally specific, they are easily translated. They are conceived in analogies, close to the original. Especially in the USA, a remake could be the result.

Still other dimensions are *international* in the sense that they have a universal appeal. International dimensions often allow directors from minor cultures to compete for foreign recognition of their oeuvres. Consequently, Hjort points to the concept of cross-filming as a dual orientation consciously helping various international audiences to appreciate a film produced by a minor film culture (1996). The dual orientation can be applied in various manners. Often a domestic orientation can be combined with a universal appeal. In this case, I would like to apply the term *domestic-universal combination strategy*. This term is used to highlight the fact that a domestic aspect doesn't need to be opaque. It can be rooted in an authentic atmosphere and combined with a universal aspect, often found in common circumstances or questions with a philosophical appeal. It can be enhanced by the application of well-known genres, myths or clusters of associations. Undertaking the balance between domestic and universal elements is a precarious matter, however, and it is not easy to tell beforehand whether it will succeed or not.

The Adaptation

When released in Denmark, *Babette's Feast* was labelled an 'illustration' of Karen Blixen, 'a respectful folk comedy, but without spirit' (Christensen 1987, p.18). As it is often the case, the literary original was enhanced and the cinematic version diminished. However, one critic has taken the opposite view. Bo Green Jensen considers the tale overestimated and praises the way in which the film visualizes the paradox of true art and the ignorant appreciation (Jensen 2002, p.88). In evaluating adaptations, questions of fidelity are unavoidable. In connection with Jane Austen's novels, Parill (2002) discusses it as the primary criterion of the audience's reaction to adaptations; just as Reynolds in his introduction to *Novel Images* take the concept of fidelity as his point of departure. Both realize that under all circumstances major changes are necessary to transfer a work of prose into a film. Discussing the process of fidelity and transfer, McFarlane draws attention to the fact that pre-modernist novels are the basis of most adaptations (McFarlane 1996, p.6). The heritage genre offers itself as a natural choice for many adaptations. When classical books are adapted, it can be done in many ways, but the costume drama can be a temptation. Higson (1996) defines the heritage genre essentially as a conservative genre, concentrated on historically attractive settings, lamenting the loss of yesterday, carried out in a slow rhythm, favouring a nostalgic reception, and he ascribes its upcoming in the 1980s to the climate in Thatcher's England.[xvii] In a Danish context, adaptations of classics or historical adaptations have been the concepts applied by film and media history.

Hjort (2003) calls for debate about the use of the heritage concept. All heritage films include national themes and have a historical dimension. They contribute to the understanding of the ways in which a society sees significant aspects of the past, which still have a bearing on contemporary identity. Hjort distinguishes between three types of Danish heritage films: 1) films that promote a nostalgic relationship to the past (e.g. *Babette's Feast* and *Barbara*), 2) films that focus on progress against the background of privation (e.g. *Pelle the Conqueror*), and 3) films that critically examine historical conditions, excluding any nostalgia (e.g. *Black Harvest*). Thus, a call for differentiation of the heritage concept is the result of Hjort's investigation of Danish heritage films produced with support from the Nordic Film and Television Foundation.

I consider *Babette's Feast* a *classical adaptation*. In Wagner's term it is 'a transposition' (1975, p.222). It exposes fidelity of transformation, which makes it a proper adaptation rather than a commentary or a parody. In this sense, it is not wrong to call it an 'illustration', but I oppose the derogatory connotation of the term. The film not only illustrates the tale; as I intend to show, it also adds qualities to it. Regarding genre, I consider the anecdote of destiny prevalent. However, I also find it illuminating to relate the concept of heritage film to *Babette's Feast*. It certainly has traits in common with the British nostalgic type, but it contains critical elements opposing it as well. In an interview by Michael Søby, Axel describes his relationship to Louis Jouvet, one of the outstanding figures in European theatre: 'Louis Jouvet aimed for naturalism, and from him I learned the importance of being faithful to your text' (Søby 2001, p.9). The concept of fidelity recurs in Ib Bondebjerg's interview where Axel states, 'The aim throughout was to be faithful to the spirit of her tale and to make it work on film. I also used a narrator so that the film viewers would be able to hear Karen Blixen's own language. [...] the words are all Karen Blixen's (Hjort and Bondebjerg 2000, p. 39). In another interview, Axel describes the process of adapting the tale in the following way:

> *I had four colours. [...] A red colour – that is the main story. A green colour – that is the side story, which supports the main story. A yellow one – that is extracting all the dialogue I can find in Karen Blixen without making a pastiche out of her text, for that is really impossible. And a blue colour – where I remove all that simply cannot be done. (Schepelern 2003, pp.15-16).*

Obviously, making adaptations work is not at all simple; but the attitude of fidelity is reconfirmed.

The film follows the tale very closely in its way of narration, its distribution of knowledge, its representation of characters and its choice of genre. This has been documented convincingly by Lothe (2000, pp.91-101). But the film also establishes its own setting, thereby underlining its relative independence. By the text: 'Karen Blixen's *Babette's Feast*', Axel pays homage to Blixen right from the beginning. Next, the sea and the land appear as the background of 'A Film by Gabriel Axel'. The camera slowly withdraws, and a few houses are seen. The chimney smoke tells us that they are inhabited. As credits are being shown, the enlarged high angle shot makes us associate God's eye in the sky. The angle of eternity is contrasted by a close up of split cod, hanging on a rack. In this way, both distance and closeness in space and time are conveyed as the film's angle of entrance. The opposition between the spiritual and the materialist aspects is caught in a glimpse. Slowly, a piano is heard, accompanying credits. The music is modern, aberrant, searching. This tonality supports the otherness of the film, compared to the tale.

As indicated by Axel, the film makes use of a voice over corresponding to the narrator in the tale. This is a well-tested means of transformation, also applied in *Out of Africa*. In these adaptations, the association to Karen Blixen, the storyteller, especially motivates it. The voice over strikes the subdued rhythm and keeps an account of time – never losing the red thread through the span of years passing: 'Once upon a time in this remote area lived two sisters…Many years later, one night in September 1871'. In both cases, the perspective of a lifetime caught in glimpses and the consequences of the choices made are the same. In this way the film follows the sense of *time* conveyed by the tale.

Comparing, it is obvious that many lines are directly imported from the tale. When Loewenhielm reaches the state of fulfilment in the end, the sentences are conveyed in the same manner in the film as in the tale, and his Swedish words echo the Dean's Danish sayings: 'Mercy and Truth, my friends, have met …Righteousness and Bliss shall kiss one another'. As the end draws near, Philippa, his pupil, conveys the sentences written by Achilles Papin in 1871 as a final ironic wisdom: 'There you will be the great artist that God meant you to be'. As in the tale, these coincidences stress the odd ways of fate and correspond to the genre – the anecdote of destiny. Consequently, the themes of *irony of fate, the ability of the artist to transform the world* and of *identity* are as important in the film as in the tale.

As mentioned before, the most spectacular change is the choice of setting. Some Danish critics considered the change from Norwegian Berlevaag into a cluster of houses on the west coast of Jutland a failure. In my opinion it is no catastrophe. In Jutland the sea represents a proper equivalent to the mountains – and religious sects flourished in Jutland during the 19th century just as they did in Norway.[xviii] Gabriel Axel's own explanation is that the Norwegian setting did not work. It resembled 'a brightly coloured toy town' (Hjort and Bondebjerg 2000, p.38), and therefore he moved it to the plain west coast of Jutland.

Compared with the tale, the film has its advantages. Axel states that 'Film language is all about reference' (Hjort and Bondebjerg 2000, p.39), and some references are really well done. The possibility to actually hear the music is such an advantage. Per Nørgaard, the modern Danish composer, who also made the music for *The Red Mantle* and *The Prince of Jutland*, composed the music. Silence is an integrated part of the soundscape. But, as Axel has remarked, silence is only heard on the background of a sound (Hjort and Bondebjerg 2000). In this case the sounds of everyday life such as the wind, the sea, the rain and the noises of a pot boiling and scrambling spoons are ever present.

But music also manifests itself in different forms. There are three kinds of music in the film: The non-diegetic music – Per Nørgaards piano compositions and two types of diegetic music. Per Nørgaard's compositions are played in a subdued and suggestive manner, rather in a minimalist fashion. It is neither fast, nor noisy. Typically, silence reigns at first. The piano does not start at once, indicating there is no haste. Art will come to people who can wait, when they least expect it.

The diegetic music is performed in two opposing ways. The pious music in honour of God sung in the church and the psalms sung in the home of the sisters stress the dimension of spiritual longing and consolation. In contrast, the music of art appeals to the senses, most clearly revealing itself in the so-called seduction duet of Mozart's *Don Juan*, sung by Philippa and Achilles Papin. Its ending 'l'amour nous uniera' (Love shall unite us) is contradicted by Philippa's decision to abandon her music lessons. We also hear the consequences. When Papin gets her letter, he immediately stops his singing – and silence is back.

The double function of the diegetic music is paralleled by the double function of another art – the art of cooking. The daily sound of the piano and the psalms parallel the daily bread offered by way of ale-and-bread-soup, and the split cod, hanging from the drying rack. The daily food can be made so-so as when the sisters prepare it themselves, or it can be well made as when Babette prepares it, but it never represents an appeal to all the senses. In contrast, a seduction by way of cooking is presented in the final French dinner thus mirroring the seduction by the opera music. Cooking is an art – and seduction by way of cooking is possible, just as it is possible to enjoy a meal without having the slightest idea of what you are eating and how it is prepared.

Another advantage of the film is that we actually watch the preparations during various phases from the arrival of the goods to the final meal. The slow cross cutting between the kitchen and the dining room enhances the connection between the art of creation and the pleasure of consuming. The transformation of the products from a state of nature into a state of deliciously appealing and arranged dishes visualizes Babette as a master. The dwelling camera supports associations of all the beautiful still-lifes, cherished in classical painting. Although her audience has to seek guidance for manners from the general, the effects are seen on the ruddy cheeks of the congregation – including the horseman who watches Babette in the kitchen, and her red-haired servant.

Combination Strategies in *Babette's Feast*

Like Blixen and Babette, Axel has the urge to demonstrate what true art is and how ungrateful audiences can be towards it – even if they enjoy it (Jensen 2002). Right from the beginning Blixen adapted her tales to a domestic-universal combination strategy. Besides, she made use of a dual language strategy to assure as large an audience as possible. It is therefore logical that Axel also chooses a domestic-universal combination strategy to reach the same purpose.

There are a few opaque elements in *Babette's Feast*. The split cod and the ale-and-bread-soup might need comments by natives. So might historical references, e.g. to Hauge, the preacher. The understanding of the tradition of the psalms might need an explanation as well. But translatable and international elements are predominant.

Translatable elements are the Danish setting and the language in which Danish, Swedish and French are included. The coastal area near the Northern Sea suggests a specific rough climate, inhibited by coarse and taciturn people, understatements being part of their nature, people who have got strong beliefs. Danes would associate to well known sects described in literature.[xix] The manners and ways of the small community are specific. Parallels can be found in any other country, however. The language (including the texts of the psalms) is specific, but it can be translated. What is difficult to translate, are the different voices in Danish, Swedish, and French. Dubbing is meaningless, as the linguistic shades would disappear. In the tale we are informed that Babette never learns to speak Norwegian properly. In the film we hear her search for words ourselves, and are convinced.

Among the most obvious international elements are the genres and the theme. Although the term anecdote of destiny was coined by Blixen as a less serious version of the tale of destiny, it is universally known in various versions from *The Bible* (cf. her 'Isak') to *Thousand and One Nights* and modern tales. The anecdote of destiny refers to a humorous topic and an ironic way of presentation, highlighting paradoxes. It relates everyday questions to philosophical issues. The combination with the heritage film gives *Babette's Feast* a mixed contemporary-historical frame of reference, following the lead from *Out of Africa* and the British heritage films in the 1980s – and commenting on them. Consequently, the story is constructed in a manner that implies surprises, and the style is classical. Thematically, the opposition between spirit and flesh, piety and vanity, aesthetics and ethics is well known, not only in Western culture. Besides, music is a universal language.

Especially the casting helps to bring together different national spheres: the French Stephane Audran as Babette is brought to communicate with the pious sisters, performed by the Danish actresses Birgitte Federspiel and Bodil Kjer – in her hesitant Danish. The Swedish Jarl Kulle contributes to the process of translation by making his Swedish very distinct and understandable to Danish audience. But it is still Swedish. The point is that different cultures are brought together, conveying different expectations and atmospheres. The issue of language is crucial in demonstrating this. In the film, the differences of languages and social spheres are heard not only in singing and music, but also via intonation and choice of words.

As pointed out formerly, the concept of 'heritage film' can be combined with the idea of a domestic-universal combination strategy. The casting makes a direct link to Carl Th. Dreyer's films, which to the international audience for many years was synonymous with Danish cinema (Le Fanu 2003; Sauvaget 2003; Nishimura 2003). In *Ordet* (1955), Birgitte Federspiel and Preben Lerdorff-Rye performed the main roles as Inger and Johannes. In *Gertrud* (1964), Ebbe Rode performed the part of Lidman. These actors convey a sense of historical depth and continuity. The beginning of the film enhances the four elements as the keynote in the depiction of the landscape: air, water, earth and fire. Though poverty is the not idyllic, charity may appeal to noble sentiments, and *Babette's Feast* also resembles a heritage film in other ways: it has a slow pace, it has a narrator, and there is a certain nostalgic attitude in the dominant resignation of Martine and Philippa. Besides, it is occupied with the debate of which values determine people's lives. But how does the anecdote of destiny correspond to the heritage genre?

In my opinion, the anecdote of destiny weakens the historical aspect and stresses the universal element. Historical circumstances may vary, times may change, but the artists' desire to create remains basically the same, just as the divine laughter when they succeed. As an anecdote, a tale can be turned upside down, and the irony inherent in the anecdote is strange to nostalgia. As opposed to this, a criticism directed against mainstreaming films such as *Out of Africa* can be traced. According to *Babette's Feast,* it is imperative to keep up artistic standards hoping that the audience will appreciate it.

Who would be longing for a time of deprivation? More specifically, one message is that all historical times are similar in one respect: artists rarely have optimal conditions, and art is rarely recognized and appreciated by the audience at the right moment. *Babette's Feast* is first and foremost an anecdote of destiny and secondarily a heritage film. Nevertheless, the heritage genre has influenced both the production and the reception.

In *Babette's Feast,* the main strategy applied is the domestic-universal combination strategy. In this way both a national audience and international audiences are addressed. It is ironic that *Out of Africa* helped to prepare both audiences for *Babette's Feast. Out of Africa* was immensely popular, especially in Denmark, and there is no doubt that it contributed to bridge the gap between film cultures.

REFERENCES

Agger, G. (1988) 'Genskrivningens Veje', in Nielsen, Hans Jørn (ed): *Kultur, Identitet og Kommunikation*, pp.71-90. Aalborg: Aalborg University Press.
Agger, G. (2001) 'National Cinema and TV Fiction in a Transnational Age', in G. Agger and J.F. Jensen (eds.) *The Aesthetics of Television*, pp.121-174. Aalborg: Aalborg University Press.
Andersen, H. and F. Lasson (1980) *Blixeniana 1980*. Copenhagen: Karen Blixen Selskabet.
Blixen, K. (1958) *Skæbne-Anekdoter*. Copenhagen: Gyldendal.
Blixen, K. (1985) *Syv Fantastiske Fortællinger*. Copenhagen: Gyldendal.
Brandstrup, P.G. and E.N. Redvall (2003) 'Fra Babettes Gæstebud til Blinkende Lygter. Internationaliseringen af Dansk Film', in A. Toftgaard and I.H. Hawkesworth (eds.) *Nationale Spejlinger*, pp.109-138. Copenhagen: Museum Tusculanum Forlag.
Christensen, J.H. (1987) 'Besøgende hos Elverdronningen', *Levende billeder* no. 6: 18-21.
Debusigne, B. (1989) *The Literary Image in Print and Film*. Thèse. Université de Nice.
Dinesen, I. (1986) *Anecdotes of Destiny*. Harmondsworth: Penguin.
Higson, A. (1997) *Waving the Flag: Constructing a National Cinema in Britain*. Oxford: Oxford University Press.
Higson, A. (2003) *English Heritage, English Cinema: Costume Drama Since 1980*. Oxford: Oxford University Press.
Hjort, M. and I. Bondebjerg (2000) *The Danish Directors: Dialogues on a Contemporary National Cinema*. Bristol: Intellect.
Hjort, M. (1996) 'Danish Cinema and the Politics of Recognition', in D. Bordwell and N. Caroll (eds.) *Post-Theory: Reconstructing Film Studies*, pp.520-532. Madison: University of Wisconsin Press.
Hjort, M. (2003) 'Tak for Musikken, Spillemand. Heritagefilm på Dansk', in A. Toftgaard and I.H. Hawkesworth (eds.) *Nationale Spejlinger*, pp.139-165. Copenhagen: Museum Tusculanum Forlag.
Jensen, B.G. (2002) *De 25 Bedste Danske Film*. Copenhagen: Rosinante, 2002.

Langbaum, R. (1964) *The Gayety of Vision: A Study of Isak Dinsen's Art*. London: Chatto & Windus.

Le Fanu, M. (2003) 'De to Tårne. Dansk Film Set fra Storbritannien', in A. Toftgaard and I.H. Hawkesworth (eds.) *Nationale Spejlinger*, pp.267-287. Copenhagen: Museum Tusculanum Forlag.

Lothe, J. (2000) *Narrative in Fiction and Film: An Introduction*. Oxford: Oxford University Press.

McFarlane, B. (1996) *Novel to Film: An Introduction to the Theory of Adaptation*. Oxford: Clarendon Press.

Nishimura, Y. (2003) 'Langt fra Danmark. Dansk Film Set fra Japan', in A. Toftgaard and I.H. Hawkesworth (eds.) *Nationale Spejlinger*, pp.305-316. Copenhagen: Museum Tusculanum Forlag.

Parill, S. (2002) *Jane Austen on Film and Television*. London: McFarland.

Reynolds, P. (1993) *Novel Images: Literature in Perfomance*. London: Routledge.

Sauvaget, D. (2003) 'Danske Fristelser. Dansk Film Set fra Frankrig', in A. Toftgaard and I.H. Hawkesworth (eds.) *Nationale Spejlinger*, pp.289-303. Copenhagen: Museum Tusculanum Forlag.

Schepelern, P. (1995) 'Mellem Lyst og Pligt: Filmkultur og Filmkritik in Danmark', *MedieKultur* 23: 5-25.

Schepelern, P. and E. Jørholt (eds.) (2001) *100 Års Dansk Film*. Copenhagen: Rosinante.

Schepelern, P. (2003) 'Så Gode Venner Var De Vist', *EKKO* 17: 13-17.

Søby, M. (2001) 'Gabriel Axel: A Life in Images', *Film* 15: 9-10.

Thurman, J. (1986) *Isak Dinesen: The Life of Karen Blixen*. Harmondsworth: Penguin.

Wagner, G.A. (1975) *The Novel and the Cinema*. Rutherford, N.J.: Fairleigh Dickinson University Press.

With, M. K. (1964) *Karen Blixen. Et udvalg*. Copenhagen: Gyldendal.

FILMS REFERENCED

Axel, G. (dir.) (1987) *Babette's Feast*. Denmark: A-S Panorama Film International.

Dreyer, C.Th. (dir.) (1955) *Ordet*. Denmark: Johan Ankerstjerne.

Dreyer, C.Th. (dir.) (1964) *Gertrud*. Denmark: Palladium.

Pollack, S. (dir.) (1985) *Out of Africa*. USA: Universal Pictures.

NOTES

[viii] In three books Wilhelm Dinesen conveyed his impressions, experiences and reflections from his participation in the war in Slesvig 1864, the German – French war in 1870, and from his years in Wisconsin during the 1870s. Merete With (1964) points out that Isak Dinesen's understanding of the relationship between civilisation and indigenous culture strikingly resembles her father's (p.183).

[ix] Established on the basis of Thurman (1986) and Langbaum (1964).

[x] Andersen & Lasson (1980) document the reception of *Seven Gothic Tales* in the USA, England, Sweden and Denmark. Karen Blixen's books were soon translated elsewhere, broadening the international aspect.

[xi] Unless otherwise indicated, all quotations with page numbers only are from the following source: Dinesen, I. (1986) *Anecdotes of Destiny*. Harmondsworth: Penguin.

[xii] 'Fifteen years later' (p. 32), but 'Sixteen years later' in the Danish edition (Blixen 1958, p.40). Consequently, the 'twelve years, until the time of this tale' (p. 35) is 'fourteen years' in the Danish edition (Blixen 1958, p.42).

[xiii] This might echo Karen Blixen's own abilities: 'I can cook, take care of mad people and write' (With 1964, p.188).

[xiv] 'Tuesday morning' in the Danish edition (Blixen 1958, p.54).

[xv] Birgitte Debusigne in *The Literary Image in Print and Film* 1989 discusses the question of Babette's identity.

[xvi] During the 1990s, Danish cinema concentrated more on contemporary films than on heritage films.

[xvii] Since 1995, when *Waving the Flag* first appeared, Higson has modified and differentiated his original presumptions.

[xviii] There are many possible Danish equivalents to the Norwegian preacher Hans Nielsen Hauge (1771 – 1824), who may be a model for the Dean.

[xix] E.g. Hans Kirk: *Fiskerne* 1928, which was adapted as a television serial in 1977.

Dickens Adaptations from *South Park* to *Futurama*

Jørgen Riber Christensen

Dickens' novels may pop-up in the most surprising places. Their intertextual potential seems to be enormous. Not only are they adapted again and again for film and television as programs and features in their own right, they also take on peculiar and unlikely forms such as science fiction, musicals, puppet film and cartoons. This chapter will concentrate on the more esoteric Dickens adaptations and examine how it is possible to adapt *Oliver Twist*, for instance, into versions where Oliver has become a dog. How have Dickens' texts become so ubiquitous and pervasive, and how is it possible for them to survive and remain recognizable?

Wanting More

The singularly best-known situation in all of Charles Dickens' works is when Oliver Twist asks for more in the poor house:

> *The evening arrived; the boys took their places. The master, in his cook's uniform, stationed himself at the copper; his pauper assistants ranged themselves behind him; the gruel was served out; and a long grace was said over the short commons. The gruel disappeared; the boys whispered to each other, and winked at Oliver; while his next neighbours nudged him. Child as he was, he was desperate with hunger, and reckless with misery. He rose from the table; and advancing to the master, basin and spoon in hand, said: somewhat alarmed at his own temerity:*
> *'Please, sir, I want some more.'*
> *The master was a fat, healthy man; but he turned very pale. He gazed in stupified astonishment on the small rebel for some seconds, and then clung for support to the copper. The assistants were paralysed with wonder; the boys with fear.*
> *'What!' said the master at length, in a faint voice.*
> *'Please, sir,' replied Oliver, 'I want some more.'*
> *The master aimed a blow at Oliver's head with the ladle; pinioned*

him in his arm; and shrieked aloud for the beadle.
The board were sitting in solemn conclave, when Mr. Bumble rushed into the room in great excitement, and addressing the gentleman in the high chair, said, 'Mr. Limbkins, I beg your pardon, sir! Oliver Twist has asked for more!'
There was a general start. Horror was depicted on every countenance.
'For MORE!' said Mr. Limbkins. 'Compose yourself, Bumble, and answer me distinctly. Do I understand that he asked for more, after he had eaten the supper allotted by the dietary?'
'He did, sir,' replied Bumble.
'That boy will be hung,' said the gentleman in the white waistcoat.
'I know that boy will be hung.' (Oliver Twist 1837-39, ch. 2)

In what may be said to be the ultimate and canonical adaptation of the novel, David Lean's *Oliver Twist* (1948), this situation is rendered rather faithfully, though the passage, 'He rose from the table; and advancing to the master, basin and spoon in hand', is given more tension than in the novel. A long shot in deep focus is used when poor Oliver walks tortuously slowly up the aisle between the tables to ask the master for more gruel. The foreground of Oliver advancing from the deep background is made up of the master's cane, which vibrates expectantly.

In Glenn Hill's *Family Guy: Let's Go to the Hop* (2000), the asking-for-more scene is inserted into the action, though not really to develop the plot, but seemingly only for the joy of intertextual recognition. This scene is altered fundamentally, however, though not beyond recognition. First of all, the scene is anchored and identified in the dialogue of the episode, when Peter Griffin says to his wife, 'Not now honey, I've got to write a book report on Oliver Twist'. The prematurely developed and domination-bent baby Stewie, who is also reading the book, interposes, 'Oliver Twit, if you ask me. I would have done things rather differently, I can tell you that', and there is a cut to what looks like the scene from Lean's film with Oliver, who has now become Stewie, walking up towards the master. Stewie, who is slightly overacting and yet seems a bit bored, speaks the lines and asks for more. The master reacts with fury, but now this adaptation becomes less than faithful, as Stewie puts down his little bowl and spoon, pulls out a large space-ray-zap-gun, points it at the Victorian master, and says, 'All right, stop it right there!' The roles of domination have now become reversed as Stewie forces the master to fill up the bowl, then put on a woman's dress. Finally, as he fires at the master's feet, Stewie commands, 'Now, dance!' In Stewie's imagination he, as all other readers since 1837, has identified with Oliver Twist, but now in an active reader-response mode. Stewie's identification with Oliver goes only this far, as Stewie as the modern nuclear-family child he is, does not accept Victorian repression, but fights back. The powerlessness of all *Oliver Twist*-readers has here been turned into a response, which is more than genre parody. Stewie's exaggerated response is not totally out of line with the emotions that the young Oliver Twist's fate has always elicited.

Another recent cartoon version of the Oliver-asking-for-more-scene can be seen in Matt Groening's *Futurama: Xmas Story* (1999). In this scene two Dickens-texts have been condensed into one. It is Christmas, and so the Tiny Tim from a *Christmas Carol* (1843) has been cast in the role of Oliver. Tiny Tim is here a small robot child with a mechanical crutch-arm. The young robot is aptly called Tinny Tim. The amoral robot, Bender, has heard that the shelter for homeless and destitute robots gives out free booze (i.e. robot food), and so, disguised as a filthy hobo, he practically empties the shelter of booze. The condensation of the scene is quite extensive. As in the case with *Family Guy*, this intertextual reuse of Dickens also rests on David Lean's 1948 film. The initial travelling camera in the scene of the paupers eating at the table in Lean's adaptation is repeated in the *Futurama* version, but here Bender has taken up Oliver's seat, with the difference that the table in front of Bender is covered with emptied bowls. In the background Tinny Tim slowly progresses towards the kind robot who dispenses the booze. The copper is empty, however, because of Bender's insatiable thirst for booze, and Tinny Tim can have none, though he asks politely, 'Excuse me, Sir, might I have a sip of booze?' The poor little robot turns away disappointedly with a tubercular cough. Bender now actually reacts with a guilty conscience, which might have seemed an unknown feeling to him: 'My God, that poor kid'. Though this version of *Oliver Twist* is drastically distanced from the original book, the emotional impact of the scene is nevertheless retained.

'Give your family a taste of classic literature', reads the videocassette cover of *Wishbone: Twisted Tail* (1995). In this thirty-minute episode in the Wishbone series for children, directed by Rick Duffield, the lead actor is a well-groomed fox terrier. In each episode of the series the dog,

Wishbone, becomes one of the great characters from canonical literature. At the same time Wishbone is living with his present-day American middle-class family, so that there is a double narrative structure where the action, characters and themes of a classical text are mirrored in suburban American life. In the *Oliver Twist* episode Wishbone has not been fed, and to forget his hunger he starts to read Dickens' classic tale. Unfortunately, the book opens on the Oliver-asking-for-more scene. Aching with hunger, Wishbone identifies with Oliver and the scene becomes a Victorian workhouse with Wishbone dressed up as Oliver and asking for more. As the main audience of the series is young children who may be encountering Dickens for the first time, this imaginative adaptation of *Oliver Twist* is anchored by Wishbone's educational voice-over: 'Hmm, 1830s-England, of course, Charles Dickens. Must be *Oliver Twist*. The perfect story for a dog alone and hungry….You see, Oliver was an orphan, which means he was a stray with no collar and no I.D. tag'. The first Victorian scene in the Wishbone episode is Oliver asking for more. As this is the best known part of *Oliver Twist* this choice may also help the audience to recognize what novel it is that is being adapted. Obviously there are certain problems connected to casting Oliver Twist as a dog. Oliver as a fox terrier may seem quite a strong *Verfremdungseffect*, especially as the dog actor is dressed up in tailor-made costumes, and the overriding mood is one of ironic detachment, where Wishbone's witty and quick voice over ensures distance between the classical text and the adaptations in the series. This distance is meant to co-exist with the proximity the episode purports there is between Dickens' socially and morally indignant novel about the inhuman effects of the Poor Law in the 1830s and problems in Suburbia in the 1990s. Fagin is left out. The Artful Dodger recruits Oliver/Wishbone in the Victorian passages of the episode, and then steals a handkerchief from Mr. Brownlow as in the novel. In the present-day passages Wishbone is only initially combined with Oliver through the feeling of hunger, and then the Oliver character is taken over by a new boy in town, Max, who like Oliver Twist is an orphan and lives in an institution. Though Max is treated well by Wishbone's family and friends, he nevertheless gets into bad company and is suspected of burglarizing some houses in the neighbourhood. (The most prominent of the stolen goods is a front garden pink plastic flamingo.) Wishbone and the children play detectives, Max is found to be innocent, and the real culprit, a present-day Artful Dodger on roller-skates, but otherwise quite anonymous, is apprehended by the police.

This ambivalent and detached adaptation of *Oliver Twist* offers facile parallels between the Victorian novel and minor problems in contemporary American middle class life. A closer reading of the asking-for-more scene points to some of the problems that arise in an adaptation that has no clear premise. The scene opens with a close-up of gruel being ladled into a tin bowl held by a pair of (human) hands. The camera tilts slightly upward as the next boy in line gets his gruel and the camera pans following the boy's progress as he walks around the table to sit down and eat. The sound is a mixture of relatively sombre underscoring and Wishbone's voice over. As we see the second boy walking around the table, Wishbone says, 'You see, Oliver was an orphan'. Wishbone's mentioning of the name Oliver in this context seems to be an identifying anchorage of the walking boy, so that the audience believes him to be Oliver Twist. However, as the boy walks behind Wishbone sitting at the table in his Victorian cap the camera pan stops and the boy walks out of the picture. Now we see Wishbone well lit, with the boys around him seated in shadow. The audience now has to revise its idea of identities in the scene. Oliver's walk towards the master to ask for more takes on quite a surprising form here. 'All right. This is it! I am a dog on a mission. Watch me boys. Follow my lead', Wishbone says, and holding his bowl in his muzzle he walks on the tabletop towards the master, jumps to the floor, coughs slightly to catch the master's attention, and speaks his lines: 'Please, Sir, I want some more. I want some more. – Hey, work with me here. Throw me a bone. Anything!' Like the dog he is, he is duly lifted up and thrown out. He does not land in a Victorian back alley, however, but in the living room of his present-day home. And so, through this jump cut Oliver Twist escapes from his situation as a Victorian pauper into present-day America. In all fairness, the novel's Oliver Twist also took a journey into the middle classes, but the point is that this journey was rather more strenuous than a facile cinematographic act.

Eisenstein, Griffith and Dickens

In his essay 'Charles Dickens' (1940) George Orwell remarked that 'Dickens is one of those writers who are well worth stealing',[xx] and the huge number of adaptations of Dickens' novels, plays and short stories indicates that Dickens is not only well worth stealing, but also that Dickens is fairly easy to appropriate and to adapt. There are good reasons why. Already in 1897 the American Mutoscope film company adapted a scene from *Oliver Twist*, 'the Death of Nancy Sykes', into a film, and the next year the British director R.W. Paul filmed 'Mr. Bumble the Beadle', also from *Oliver Twist*. Since then it is has been hard to keep track of the number of adaptations.[xxi] Not only film producers are indebted to Dickens, film theorists are as well. In 'Dickens, Griffith and the Film Today' Sergei Eisenstein (1949) states his own and D.W. Griffith's indebtedness to Dickens' narrative techniques. Dickens' visual style, his use of details and his cutting of long narrative stretches into scenes have influenced the montage technique of film, and Griffith's use of close-ups. For instance, the structural device of cross-cutting as it is used in Griffith's *Intolerance* is similar to Dickens' moving from one scene to the next in his novels. Eisenstein's key points are that Dickens' narrative technique is in many ways cinematic and that Griffith's narrative form was influenced by Dickens. Eisenstein claims that in the end the revolutionary Soviet film superseded Griffith and also indirectly Dickens.

Dickens was the first modern urban writer who wrote for a mass audience. Eisenstein mentions that Dickens' audience was not unlike a modern film audience. Today one may add television audience, as Dickens' serial form of publication by instalment made his novels particularly suited for adaptations into television series with the interrupted viewing of each episode, just as the character based plots of the novels go well into the television form. Dickens' narrative form has many characteristics that can easily be transferred to film. The time structure as seen in *A Christmas Carol*, with flashbacks and flash-forwards, has become a cinematic narrative cliché. The cliffhangers at the end of an instalment in Dickens' novels can be found in film and in television series. The narrative pattern of Dickens' fiction may be compared with the structure of a well-cured and striped piece of bacon, i.e. alteration between slow and fast passages, romantic and sorrowful ones, and intimate and panoramic ones. These narrative patterns presage cinematographic crosscutting. Eisenstein stresses Dickens' almost uncanny perceptive power and his ability to evoke the sounds and smells of street life in London and of Londoners, and praises Dickens' texts for their optical quality, which again and again illustrates details of London life. Eisenstein argues that this optical narrative technique is a forerunner for the cinematographic ultra-close-up and close-up.

Griffith used narrative forms straight out of Dickens including parallel action, montage clips, dynamic montage, and speed as an increase of tempo in the montage. He employed montage as progression of parallel scenes, which were intercut into each other, and also digressions to create suspense. This is what Eisenstein calls the disjunctive method of narration. Griffith's use of the close-up is a special point. Although Griffith did not invent the close-up, his predecessors never used them as consistently to advance the narrative. Griffith's method of employing close-ups at dramatic climaxes was a cinematic innovation.

Eisenstein is critical of Griffith, and also indirectly of Dickens. Both Dickens and Griffith used the parallel montage ideologically to create a hypothetical reconciliation in the end. Eisenstein argues that the parallel montage is a reflection of a dualist world picture consisting of the poor and the rich. The two lines of parallel montage will only cross in infinity 'just as inaccessible as that "reconciliation"'(Eisenstein 1949, p.235). Reconciliation or merging is not the same as the creation of a new unity that Eisenstein finds in the Soviet revolutionary montage of attractions, e.g. *Strike* (1925).

Another Soviet critic, Mikhail Bakhtin, deflects some of the criticism of Dickens through his description of another kind of montage found in the novels of Dickens. This type of montage, heteroglossia, is the multiplicity of voices, styles, idiolects and sociolects within one text so that one voice always has a dialogic relationship to the other voices (1981). (Or, to put it another way, there are combinations of discourses.) This presence of many voices has a disruptive effect and in Dickens this stylistic disruption usually has a comic and satirical function. When several sociolects are used together and the social hierarchies are inverted through this mixture of voices from different social strata the effect is carnivalesque and the social order is questioned ideologically.

What is it in Dickens that makes it possible to transform his texts without destroying them? We have seen in the first pages of this chapter how *Oliver Twist* has been reformulated into *Family Guy*, *Futurama* and *Wishbone*. These intertextual references to the novel and also to previous adaptations of it are somewhat esoteric, yet they are recognizable, and each of them functions at its own level. The answer to the question above requires that we return to an argument about the presence of formal qualities in Dickens that has raged since the first publication of his novels. There are two poles in the critical response to Dickens. At one pole are the formalists who see Dickens' novels as violations of the novel genre. Formalists like Henry James focus on Dickens' additive plots, his digressions, and his perpetual introduction of new characters. New Critics seek to show that there is after all structural unity in Dickens' works. Those at the exuberance pole view Dickens' whole production as the salient point, i.e. the sheer excessiveness and scope of his fictional world. The reader is time after time overwhelmed by the magnitude of the settings, the number of characters, the emotional overload, and the extravagance and excess of language. Although these critical responses have polarized criticism of Dickens, both poles agree that Dickens' texts have an open quality. His novels are not just open in the sense that they are amenable to various reader interpretations. They are also open in their design and production process, for example when new characters and subplots are introduced or when heteroglossia creates a polyphonic chorus of different voices. The excess of language and characters and character descriptions, the overwhelming amount of detail, and the emotional overload all allow a formal instability, which ignores boundaries and closures, and it is this openness that invites yet another new and excessive version of Dickens' novels. A power-mad baby with a ray gun, a robot, and a fox terrier with a cap are allowed within the universe of *Oliver Twist*, which itself has so many excesses that a few more make no difference to the core text.

South Park Classics and *Great Expectations*

> *British Person:*
> *'Ahhhh Dickens. The imagery of cobblestone streets, craggy London buildings and nutmeg filled Yorkshire puddings. Hello. I'm a British person. For years now the character Pip has been featured prominently in the American show South Park. However many Americans don't realize where Pip came from. He's the prowling, adorable little Englishman from Charles Dickens' timeless classic 'Great Expectations'. And so tonight the makers of South Park have agreed to take a break from their regular show and instead present the prestigious Dickens tale in its entirety from beginning to end. Indeed after watching this show you'll know the timeless classic as if you read the Cliff Notes themselves. Our story is set in England in the small town of Draftherdshire upon Topsmart. Where a young blond haired boy named Pip was on the way to see his parents'.*

This is the actor Malcolm McDowell's introduction to South Park's cartoon adaptation of *Great Expectations*. 🙢 *Great Expectations* was Dickens' thirteenth novel. It was published in the magazine *All the Year Round* from December 1860 to August 1861. The story is told in the first person by Pip looking back in disillusion on his life and his development into a gentleman. Pip is one of the deepest of Dickens' main characters, with more personality and self-awareness than seen before in the novels. As with *Oliver Twist*, David Lean has created an adaptation that has become the benchmark for all later productions. Lean's *Great Expectations* (1946) may be regarded as the best of all Dickens adaptations, with his *Oliver Twist* as the second best. A problem with the adaptation of *Great Expectations* could have been how to render both Pip the Unreformed and Pip the Reformed, who is the narrator of the novel. The choice was to use voice over to denote the presence of Pip the Reformed, while watching the young Pip. Some plot elements and characters were removed. Orlick is gone, so that Mrs. Joe dies earlier and from natural causes. Herbert's romance with Clara and his financial dependence on Pip have been omitted. A few elements were added to the film that were not in the novel. Pip tears down the old, rotten curtains at Satis House and Estella is seated in Miss Havisham's chair. The *mise-en-scene* of the film is highly successful. It recreates the grotesque and Gothic nature of scenes in the novel, as for instance its climax with Miss Havisham burning, so that the film may be said to add something to its source text. 🙢

In the face of the canonical Lean adaptation it is courageous, if not foolhardy, for the *South Park* series to enter into competition with the good taste of this successful British film. From the first seconds of *South Park: Great Expectations* (2000) the discourse is one about taste. In particular, contemporary popular American taste (viz. South Park) is contrasted with the cultural heritage stemming from Britain. Malcolm McDowell, after having introduced himself as 'a British person', seeks ironically to tie the two cultures together. Using McDowell as a link between 'Dickens' timeless classic', as he calls *Great Expectations*, and the South Park version is symptomatic of the narrative structure found in postmodern pastiches, which in their popular recreations of classics possessing copious cultural capital have to navigate between two value systems. In *South Park: Great Expectations* the solution is metafictional as McDowell's introduction is a paratext that not only anchors the identity of the episode, but also foregrounds the question of the transatlantic dichotomy of taste. *South*

Park: Great Expectations is a pastiche, but with satirical elements. These elements are not so much directed against the source text itself as against its annexation by a literary and academic establishment that has reduced the popular writer Charles Dickens into CliffsNotes[xxii]. In *American Notes for General Circulation* (1842) Dickens cannot be said to be kind to Americans and their lack of taste when he describes the habit of spitting:

> THE journey from New York to Philadelphia, is made by railroad, and two ferries; and usually occupies between five and six hours. It was a fine evening when we were passengers in the train: and watching the bright sunset from a little window near the door by which we sat, my attention was attracted to a remarkable appearance issuing from the windows of the gentleman's car immediately in front of us, which I supposed for some time was occasioned by a number of industrious persons inside, ripping open feather-beds, and giving the feathers to the wind. At length it occurred to me that they were only spitting, which was indeed the case; though how any number of passengers which it was possible for that car to contain, could have maintained such a playful and incessant shower of expectoration, I am still at a loss to understand: notwithstanding the experience in all salivatory phenomena which I afterwards acquired...
> One of two remarkable circumstances is indisputably a fact, with reference to that class of society who travel in these boats. Either they carry their restlessness to such a pitch that they never sleep at all; or they expectorate in dreams, which would be a remarkable mingling of the real and ideal. All night long, and every night, on this canal, there was a perfect storm and tempest of spitting; and once my coat, being in the very centre of the hurricane sustained by five gentlemen (which moved vertically, strictly carrying out Reid's Theory of the Law of Storms), I was fain the next morning to lay it on the deck, and rub it down with fair water before it was in a condition to be worn again...
> Nobody says anything, at any meal, to anybody. All the passengers are very dismal, and seem to have tremendous secrets weighing on their minds. There is no conversation, no laughter, no cheerfulness, no sociality, except in spitting.[xxiii]

The use of bodily abjects is a defining characteristic of the humour of *South Park* (e.g. Mr. Hankey the Christmas Poo), and the pattern holds in *South Park: Great Expectations*. Initially the episode is quite faithful to the novel, though both plot and the number of characters have been substantially reduced. Near the end of the episode great liberties are taken, as it appears that Miss Havisham has built a Genesis device that uses the tears of all Estella's rejected boyfriends as fuel. The Genesis device will enable her to gain revenge on the male race, and she and Estella will be fused. This transformation of the genre from Gothic melodrama and *Bildungsroman* to science fiction is accompanied by Miss Havisham's army of robot monkeys. But despite these evil creatures Joe, Magwitch, Herbert and Pip manage to fight them off and convince Estella that she has a heart. Mrs. Havisham dies in a fire in the Genesis device, and Pip and Estella live happily ever after. *South Park: Great Expectations* is full of excesses within the action of the episode itself. In its paratexts it is also quite a complex metafictional discourse about taste and the relationship between a pastiche and its source text.

Mickey Mouse, the Muppets, Mr. Magoo and the Flintstones

Just as *Oliver Twist* and *Great Expectation* have their classic adaptations, so Brian Desmond directed the definitive film version of *A Christmas Carol* (1843) with Alastair Sim as curmudgeon reborn in *Scrooge* (1951). More recent versions of *A Christmas Carol* seem to be as much intertextual and metafictional projects as clear-cut adaptations. They may quote *Scrooge* or other films or even include Charles Dickens himself as an author persona who becomes a character in his own text. In *The X-Files* adaptation entitled 'How the Ghosts Stole Christmas' (1998), *Scrooge* is quoted both directly and indirectly. The main part of the episode takes place in an old, allegedly haunted house the night before Christmas, into which Agent Mulder (David Duchovny) lures Agent Scully (Lilian Anderson). Here they meet a ghostly couple who appear every Christmas night since their double suicide on Christmas 1917. These ghosts are not as benevolent as the ghosts in *A Christmas Carol*. In fact they seek, in vain, to make Scully and Mulder kill one another. The end of the episode shows Mulder alone in his flat celebrating Christmas by watching television; on the screen is *Scrooge* with Alastair Sim . The fact that *Scrooge* is quoted directly near the end of the episode is not the only intertextual clue. The presence of ghosts on Christmas night is sufficient to point to Dickens. Dickensian benevolence is not totally absent from this Gothic tale as Scully comes uninvited and interrupts Mulder's lonely Christmas. They exchange presents, which they had purchased in anticipation of a fortuitous meeting. The way *A Christmas Carol* is used in this episode of *The X-Files* illustrates degree to which *A Christmas Carol* has become a pivotal cultural text and a part of the rituals surrounding Christmas.

In *The Muppet Christmas Carol* (1992) the Great Gonzo has the role as Dickens himself, who is introduced as both a narrator and 'a nineteenth-century novelist, a genius'. The Great Gonzo (as Dickens) introduces the story, and as the author is present, so the audience also has its representative on screen in the form of Rizzo the Rat, who once in a while interrupts the narration with untimely questions. A human actor in the role as Scrooge supplements the metafictional devices so that the presence of Michael Caine among the Muppets functions as a further *Verfremdungseffect*. It may seem that the familiarity that the audience is expected to have with both the plots and the characters of this well-known Dickens text makes it necessary to tell the story in a new and original way, at the same time as the textuality of the story is stressed. Despite its metafictional licence the Muppet pastiche of *A Christmas Carol* does not in any way destroy the mother text, and the same may perhaps surprisingly be said to be the case with another fairly recent version. Richard Boden's *Blackadder's Christmas Carol* (1988) is saturated with the bilious and satirical remarks of Blackadder, yet the show is not strictly a parody of Dickens' original text. The initially benevolent Ebeneezer Blackadder turns into the greedy Scrooge prototype after having been shown scenes from his vile forefathers' history by the Spirit of Christmas. But *Blackadder's Christmas Carol* is intertextually just as much connected to the Blackadder television series as to Dickens' *A Christmas Carol*. Rowan Atkinson is just as much Blackadder as he is Ebenezer Scrooge, and quite long scenes from the historical epochs of the various Blackadder series make up the film clips that the Spirit of Christmas shows to Ebenezer Blackadder. Even two *Dr. Who* parodies are included, and it is typical of this television episode that the parodic elements are not so much of Dickens as of the historical costume film genre in general, typically parodied throughout the Blackadder series. The familiarity that any television audience has with *A Christmas Carol* is turned to good use; *Blackadder's Christmas Carol* as a whole is a parody of clichés from the multitude of Dickens television productions, in particular all the other adaptations of *A Christmas Carol*.

The metafiction of Burney Mattinson's *Mickey's Christmas Carol* (1983) is a question of distribution. In itself this adaptation follows the Dickens text quite closely, with the various Disney characters as the cast. Goofy is Marley's ghost, and obviously Scrooge McDuck is Scrooge. Carl Barks, the creator of Scrooge McDuck, based his cartoon character on Ebenezer Scrooge. Scrooge McDuck first appeared in the comic strip story 'Christmas on Bear Mountain' in 1947. The metafiction is paratextual as *Mickey's Christmas Carol* today is distributed on the DVD *Mickey's Magical Christmas: Snowed In at the House of Mouse* from 2001. Here *Mickey's Christmas Carol* is just one out of a number of cartoon shorts shown by Mickey Mouse to his various Disney character guests, who have to spend Christmas in his night club-like movie theatre as they are snowed in there. *House of Mouse* was a series on the Disney Channel running from 2001 to 2003. *Mickey's Christmas Carol* is in other words contextualised by Mickey as the emcee. The reformation of Scrooge is reflected in the paratexts where Donald Duck as part of the audience initially does not possess the Christmas spirit, mostly because of his star rivalry with Mickey Mouse. It is not until Donald Duck realized that Mickey is his best friend that Donald stops saying 'Humbug!' and *Mickey's Christmas Carol* can be shown.

The tradition with reusing a cast in adaptations of *A Christmas Carol* as it was seen above in *The Muppet Christmas Carol*, *Blackadder's Christmas Carol* and *Mickey's Christmas Carol* includes Mr. Magoo and the Flintstones. In *Mr. Magoo's Christmas Carol* from 1962 the core text, *A Christmas Carol*, is again adapted within a paratextual context. The changes in the core text are primarily that originally created songs have been inserted. The paratext is the production of a Broadway musical in which Mr. Magoo stars as Scrooge. The prelude of this one-hour cartoon is the myopic Mr Magoo's catastrophic drive through New York to the theatre and his just as catastrophic entry into the theatre. During the prelude a newspaper headline, 'Critics laud Magoo's "Carol"', is displayed and on the theatre billboard it says, 'Quincy Magoo stars in A Christmas Carol'. During the production of *A Christmas Carol* the theatre audience is glimpsed a few times. But apart from this, *A Christmas Carol* remains practically untouched by the paratext. For instance a duet between Bob Cratchit and Scrooge is depicted in split-screen, omitting the theatre setting completely. However, during the applause and the encores in the theatre, Mr. Magoo characteristically brings the house down, literally. There is no thematic connection between the core text and the paratext, and the connection created by their sharing of the character Mr. Magoo is quite slight as Mr. Magoo as Scrooge does not create the usual havoc.

Joanna Romersa's *A Flintstones Christmas Carol* from 1994 has the same narrative structure as *Mr. Magoo's Christmas Carol*. The Bedrock Community Players, with Wilma Flintstone as the stage manager, is going to put on a production of Charles Brickens's *A Christmas Carol*. Fred Flintstone is the leading actor going to play the role of Ebenezer Scrooge. The production of *A Christmas Carol* is the narrative frame around Dickens' core text. In *Mr. Magoo's Christmas Carol* these two narrative tiers only shared the character Mr. Magoo, who was not even himself in *The Christmas Carol* on stage. In *A Flintstones Christmas Carol* the two tiers are connected by a conflict between them, as Fred Flintstone neglects his daughter Pebbles because of his ham-like attitude to his performance: 'There can only be one Scrooge', he says to his supporting actors, and he finds it hard to do his job properly and to function socially because of the upcoming play. In fact, Fred Flintstone has forgotten it is Christmas, and he has bought no presents for his family. The parallels between the unreformed Scrooge and the (cartoon) actor playing him are striking, and *The Christmas Carol* itself is performed in the world of the Flintstones with dinosaurs and all. Barney Rubble is Cragit (Cratchit) doing his books on stone slates with hammer and chisel. Wilma Flintstone understudies various roles for actors suffering from the Bedrock bug and further links are made between the frame story and the play itself when Wilma carries her worries about Fred into the play. During the many intermissions, the parallels between the play and the frame story are even made explicit in dressing room conversations, so that the two worlds are didactically connected. As Scrooge in the play is gradually reformed, so is Fred Flintstone in his own world. *A Flintstones Christmas Carol* is an adaptation of Dickens' original text, and it is also a reformulation of it, so that a new version is created, in which both *A Christmas Carol* and The Flintstones retain their separate identities.

Folk-tale Motifs, Barthes and Dickens

Family Guy, Futurama, Wishbone, South Park, The X-Files, The Muppets, Mickey Mouse, Mr. Magoo and *The Flintstones* – all have made their versions and adaptations of a Dickens text, and yet Dickens survives and is clearly recognizable. To some extent most of these adaptations anchor their versions in paratexts and other introductions to ensure that the audience will know that it is watching a Dickens adaptation, or at least an intertextual reference to a Dickens text. This kind of anchorage is hardly necessary, and at a closer inspection the anchorage is not so much included to identify the adaptations with a label saying, 'This is Dickens', as it is a way of borrowing cultural capital from the canonical Dickens in order to raise the value of adaptations that are well within the domain of popular culture. In all the adaptations and intertextual quotes examined in this chapter there is no doubt that the references are to Dickens, and one can ask how it is possible for Dickens to survive in adaptations that are so far away from the original texts?

In the early structuralist or formalist surveys of the folktale genre in the 1920s and 1930s thousands of different folktales and their many versions from all over the world were systematized by identifying their smallest recognizable elements and placing them in an index. These elements are called motifs, and when they are collected and compared, groups of them show affinities. In *The Folktale* and *Motif-Index of Folk-Literature* Stith Thompson has described and catalogued the folktale motifs. A motif is loosely defined as the smallest element in a tale that is strong enough to survive in the (oral) tradition during the centuries with their countless retellings (1977, p.425). It gets its narrative strength from possessing something striking and unusual about it which distinguishes it from neighbouring motifs. One separate motif may be found in several folk tales, and most folktales are made up of several motifs. The motifs fall in three groups: Characters (e.g. the cruel stepmother), action elements (e.g. a giant beanstalk), and dramatic incidents (e.g. finding of a treasure). Stith Thompson's six-volume index of folktale motifs was simplified or concentrated by Vladimir Propp into only 31 functions (e.g. the hero leaves home). There are of course folk or fairy tale elements in Charles Dickens' novels. Oliver Twist is a foundling, for instance, but the recognizability even today of episodes, characters and incidents from Charles Dickens' enormous Victorian production may be partly due to the fact that many of the elements from Dickens' fiction possess the narrative strength of a folk tale motif. The linguistic and emotional excess that characterizes Dickens' style may well cause this strength. Frequent repetitions are also part of the persistence of a motif, and here Charles Dickens' enduring popularity in itself may have the effect that his characters and some of the situations in his fiction have turned into motifs. There may also be more external causes. It may be that there is a movement from text into ideology when we are dealing with Charles Dickens. Fiction may have been transformed into culture texts that have achieved an ontological function. The connotations produced in the individual reader of a Dickens text have somehow become generalized into societal myths (Barthes 1972). The role of Charles Dickens as a mouthpiece of his age and as a central cultural force with unrivalled popularity in all social classes may account for the movement from connotation to myth or ideology, and secondarily for the persistence of the identity of incidents and characters in his fiction, which makes them survive in all kinds of adaptations.

REFERENCES
Bakhtin, M. (1981) *The Dialogic Imagination: Four Essays*. Austin: University of Texas Press.
Barthes, R. (1972) *Mythologies*. London: Jonathan Cape.
Christensen, J.R. (2000) *Charles Dickens CD-ROM*. Århus: Systime.
Christensen, J.R. (1998) *Fairy Tales*. Copenhagen: Gyldendal.
Eisenstein, S. (1949) 'Dickens, Griffith and the Film Today' in S. Eisenstein and J. Leyda (ed. and trans.) *Film Form: Essays in Film Theory*, pp.195-225. New York: Harcourt, Brace & World.
Fawcett, F.D. (1952) *Dickens the Dramatist on Stage, Screen, and Radio*. London: Allen.
Glavin, J. (ed.) (2003) *Dickens on Screen*. Cambridge: Cambridge University Press.
Pointer, M. (1996) *Charles Dickens on the Screen: The Film, Television, and Video Adaptations*. Lanham, MD: Scarecrow Press.
Propp, V. (1968) *Morphology of the Folktale*. Austin: University of Texas Press.
Thompson, S. (1977) *The Folktale*. Berkeley: University of California Press.
Thompson, S. (1956) *Motif-Index of Folk-Literature: A Classification of Narrative Elements in Folktales, Ballads, Myths, Fables, Mediaeval Romances, Exempla, Fabliaux, Jest-Books, and Local Legends*. Bloomington, IN: Indiana University Press.
Zambrano, A.L. (1976) *Dickens and Film*. New York: Gordon Press.

MEDIA REFERENCED
Boden, R. (dir.) (1988) *Blackadder's Christmas Carol*. UK: BBC.
Carter, C. (1998) *The X-Files: How the Ghosts Stole Christmas #6X08*.
Craig, T., R. Gannaway, and R. Schneider (dirs.) (2001) *Mickey's Magical Christmas: Snowed In at the House of Mouse*. USA: Walt Disney Corp.
Desmond, B.H. (dir.) (1951) *Scrooge*. UK: Renown Pictures Corporation, Ltd.
Duffield, R. (1995) *Wishbone™ Twisted Tail Inspired by Charles Dickens' Oliver Twist*. USA: Big Feats! Entertainment.

Groening, M. (1999) *Futurama: Xmas Story*. USA: Twentieth Century Fox Television.
Henson, B. (dir.) (1992) *The Muppet Christmas Carol*. USA: Disney Corp.
Hill, G. (2000) *Family Guy: Let's Go to the Hop*. USA: 20th Century Fox.
Lean, D. (dir.) (1946) *Great Expectations*. UK: Rank.
Lean, D. (dir.) (1948) *Oliver Twist*. UK: Rank.
Levitow, A. (dir.) (1962) *Mr. Magoo's Christmas Carol*. USA: UPA Pictures Inc.
Romersa, J. (dir.) (1994) *A Flintstones Christmas Carol*. USA: Hanna-Barbera Productions, Inc.
Stough, E. (2000) *South Park: Great Expectations*. USA: Comedy Central.

NOTES

[xx] Orwell, "Charles Dickens" in Christensen, 2000, 'Critical Library'.

[xxi] A search in The Internet Movie Database (http://www.imdb.com/name/nm0002042/), August 2004, had 183 hits with Charles Dickens as writer. In comparison there were 22 hits with Jane Austen as writer.

[xxii] On the Cliff Notes website (http://www.cliffsnotes.com/product.asp?prod_id=4120 as consulted August 12, 2004) the booklet is presented in this way:

> *Wealth, happiness, and the valuable lessons of life envelop a varied collection of characters in Dickens' Great Expectations. Told from an orphaned boy's take on the world around him, this first-person perspective gives readers a detailed look at Victorian England – with its view of virtues and economic change. Travel back with CliffsNotes on Great Expectations to those times as you freshen up your understanding of Charles Dickens' best work with insights into themes of good and evil, plots that twist and turn, and people who want for means to make sense of their lives. Get into English literature – and the good graces of your teachers – with a classroom companion that can meet all your expectations!*

[xxiii] Dickens, *American Notes*, in Christensen, 2000, 'Critical Library'.

Teening Shakespeare

Michael Skovmand

'Teening Shakespeare' has become a major Hollywood pastime in recent years. The term 'teening' itself has as much to do with producing films with a teenage audience in mind as it has to do with employing youthful actors. In the following I will take a critical look at four recent 'youthful' film productions based on plays by Shakespeare. They are *O* (dir. Tim Blake Nelson, 2001), *Hamlet* (dir. Michael Almereyda, 2000), *10 Things I Hate About You* (dir. Gil Junger, 1999), and *Romeo + Juliet* (dir. Baz Luhrmann, 1996). In addition I look back at the first major teen Shakespeare film production, Franco Zeffirelli's *Romeo and Juliet* (1968). The term itself, 'teening', in the context of these films, is doubly problematic. We must examine the transformation of a Shakespeare play into a film on the one hand, and on the other hand, the specific targeting of a Shakespeare film towards an implied youthful audience. Both of these operations traditionally have been seen as potentially reductive, if not an outright 'dumbing down' of Shakespeare's themes and dialogue. In the article 'Totally Clueless?' (1997) Lynda Boose and Richard Burt propose to analyse the relationship between Shakespeare and Hollywood in the 1990s. In it they point to a concrete nexus between the process of popularisation in general and what they term 'youth culture':

> *Dealing with specifically filmic reproductions or appropriations of Shakespeare means that "the popular" must be thought through not only the media and institutions in which Shakespeare is now produced – mass culture, Hollywood, celebrity, tabloid – but above all, youth culture. For as Shakespeare becomes part of pop culture and Shakespearean criticism (especially film criticism) follows suit, both move into an arena increasingly driven by a specifically youth culture, and Hollywood has clearly picked up on that fact. (p. 17)*

To the extent that the area of Shakespeare studies shifts towards encompassing these cultural practices, the methodological emphasis will increasingly shift towards a cultural studies approach that includes an understanding of the role of music among many other cinematic aspects, and involves an awareness of a cinematic intertextuality which reaches far beyond the traditions of Shakespearean films. Rather than develop in-depth readings of the films, this chapter will accordingly focus on their 'kinship relations' (Jerslev 1999) to other generically related films, or to phenomena within contemporary (American) culture in a broader sense.

Youthful Remediations

Baz Luhrmann's iconic *William Shakespeare's Romeo + Juliet* (1996) has established itself as the inevitable point of reference for any discussion of 'teenage Shakespeare films'. Yet it is far from typical of the genre. In fact, both in terms of production values and style, it could almost be said to be *sui generis*. As James Loehlin points out:

> *Along with its effective plundering of youth culture and its aggressive marketing towards a teenage audience, it employs post-modern aesthetic strategies that set it off from the substantial body of teen-star-crossed-lovers films from which it derives. Luhrmann's flashy, eclectic visual style and ultra-hip ironies earmark* William Shakespeare's Romeo + Juliet *as* fin-de-siecle *spectacle. (2000, p.121)*

William Shakespeare's R+J 💿 is replete with explicit, implicit and un-acknowledged intertextualities and family resemblances (observe the irreverent plus-sign combined with the demonstrative attribution of the play to Shakespeare – two messages deliberately at cross purposes). An obvious point of comparison and contrast is Franco Zeffirelli's *Romeo and Juliet* (1968). Arguably the first teenage Shakespeare film ever to be produced, it is sometimes dubbed '*The Graduate* Shakespeare' referring to Mike Nichols' 1967 film starring Dustin Hoffman (a fairly un-rebellious point of identification for the so-called 'rebellious 1960s generation'). Superficially, Zeffirelli's and Luhrman's films seem aeons apart. Luhrmann employs extreme foregrounding of a vast array of cinematic devices and incessant intertextual winks and nudges at TV series, MTV, and the

Shakespeare canon to advertise the 'post-modernity' of *R+J* and emphasize the distance between his technique and the classical Hollywood tradition of invisible editing. Zeffirelli uses a conventional setting in a touristy Renaissance Italy, complete with period tights and dresses for his *Romeo and Juliet*, and the film is unusual mainly in its casting of two very young and inexperienced actors in the main parts. Zeffirelli, however, faced the same problem as Luhrmann: how do you get young actors, with little or no experience in Shakespearean acting to speak the blank verse convincingly? Both directors used the same strategy – cutting the long speeches drastically and substituting visuals for descriptive verse. This tactic also addressed the inherent 'problem' in *Romeo and Juliet*, which is a recurring issue in Shakespearean drama, namely the 'improbability' of young characters being capable of expressing themselves in long, rhetorically and metaphorically complex speeches of blank verse. The fact that Shakespearean characters have dramatic functions that go beyond psychologically expressing themselves convincingly, e.g., choric or deictic functions, is a general issue in film versions of Shakespeare which aim to represent characters as consistently motivated and remaining within the diegesis of the drama. But it is aggravated in teenage Shakespearean films, where classic adolescent issues of finding one's adult identity and seeking independence from parents and other socialising agencies call for narratives of evolving selves and childhood experiences.

The repertoire of cinematic foregrounding in *R+J* involves a range of subtle intertextual references, as Loehlin points out (2000, pp.122-23). Leonardo di Caprio, as Romeo, echoes James Dean's Jim Stark in Nicholas Ray's *Rebel Without a Cause* (1955), both in terms of body language, and by 'playing chicken' in speeding cars. The Anglo and Latino gangs of Montagues and Capulets reprise characterizations in *West Side Story* (1961), the musical inspired by *Romeo and Juliet*. Interestingly, both Zeffirelli and Luhrmann share a sense of *mise en scene* which is more theatrical than cinematic. Zeffirelli, with his roots in opera, retains a structure of static settings such as the town square, which calls to mind large operatic *mises en scene*. Luhrmann, particularly in the scenes in the broken-down theatre near the beach, introduces settings of deliberate theatrical artificiality which recall *the mises en scene* of his earlier film *Strictly Ballroom* from 1992, a style which was to be developed further in *Moulin Rouge!* (2001).

Michael Skovmand

Gil Junger's *10 Things I Hate About You* (1999) 🎬 is a very different Shakespeare-teening project than both Zeffirelli's and Luhrmann's. None of Shakespeare's original text from *The Taming of the Shrew* has been kept, and the Italian-based story of Katherine, the unruly woman, and Petrucchio, the mercenary tamer, has been transformed into an American high school comedy. The Shakespearean plot is simple enough: the two sisters, Katherine and little sister Bianca, live under the injunction from their father that pretty Bianca cannot marry before shrewish Katherine has found a husband. Enter wild man Petrucchio, who 'tames' Katherine in a series of violent verbal and physical encounters. The final banquet scene, with 'tamed Katherine' delivering a speech on the virtues of submissive wives, has engendered a history of feminist critical contortions, and has often been performed with a nudge and a wink, although ambiguously so in the most famous film version, Zeffirelli's *The Taming of the Shrew* (1967) starring Elizabeth Taylor and Richard Burton. *10 Things I Hate About You*, starring Julia Stiles and Australian Heath Ledger (indicating Australia's signifying function as the new 'New Frontier' in Hollywood), translates Shakespeare's unpsychologised male chauvinist fantasy into adolescent high school romance with complications (Shakespeare's comedy is actually a play within a play, with a so-called 'Induction'). Kat and Bianca, living with their overly protective single father, live under a teenage version of the Shakespearean injunction: Bianca cannot date unless Kat does. And Kat, having had her share of insensitive boyfriends, will not. Newly arrived Patrick (Ledger) is persuaded – in fact paid – to date Kat by boys having designs on Bianca. Deceptions are followed by discoveries, the unlikely couples fall in love. Superficial Bianca learns that there are more valuable things in life than Prada backpacks, and anti-social Kat learns to open up. Junger has dramatised the traditional high school dichotomies of nerds and jocks, of introverts and extroverts, of popularity versus sincerity. The time-honoured dramatic principle that sex is (potentially) funny and love is not applies to *10 Things*. The comedy is mainly relegated to the secondary characters: the gynaecologist father, the sex-obsessed female student counselor, etc.

Shifting Expectations in Cinematic Shakespeare

The transformations undertaken from *The Taming of the Shrew* to *10 Things* cannot be viewed as a 'dumbing down' of Shakespeare's play. *Shrew*, one of Shakespeare's early comedies, does not exhibit the linguistic sophistication of *Love's Labours' Lost*, or the thematic complexity of *The Merchant of Venice*. It is a robust sex farce, in which the battle between the sexes is taken to extraordinary and politically incorrect lengths. I find myself in disagreement with Richard Burt's analysis of *10 Things*:

> *A conservative idealization of the good girl. The film neuters Shakespeare's play, taking a Nancy Reagan-like 'just say No' position on the problems said by conservatives and reactionaries to have been caused or at least exacerbated by the high divorce rate in the U.S., namely, premarital teen sex, teen drinking, and teen smoking. We never see two couples consummate their relationship...* 10 Things *also enlists Shakespeare's cultural authority in the service of exclusively heterosexual romance. Bianca makes it clear to Cameron that Kat is not a lesbian... Cameron [Bianca's boyfriend-to-be] says to Patrick that he and Michael are buddies but not in 'a prison movie kinda way'.* (2002a, pp.214-15)

Actually, the film neither adopts a 'just say No' position towards sex, nor a 'sex is good for you' position. Kat has had a disappointing relationship with Joey (who now wants Bianca), and the plot of the film is really not about the *taming*, but about the emotional *thawing* of Kat. As pointed out by Burt (2002a, p.214), the film inverts the taming process: it may be about the thawing of the shrew, but it is equally about the taming or domestication of male desire, more specifically the desire of Petrucchio/Patrick.

Comedy, as Northrop Frye (1957) has taught us, is about the avoidance of pain, and Shakespeare does not invite us to speculate on the reasons for Katherine's shrewishness (which has not stopped critics from doing so). High school movies such as *10 Things*, grounded in American sub-Freudian notions of upbringing and adolescence, combine the two major strands of the comedic genre. On the one hand we experience comedy as a satire of hypocrisy and rigidity with all the ridiculousness of 'the old community'. On the other hand, we see comedy as a celebration of the formation of a 'new community' of youth and love. *10 Things* manages to negotiate this doubleness as it combines the romance of identity formation and the finding of soul-mates with the satirical comedy of stereotypical parents, teachers, and the predictable range of adolescent card-board characters (geeks, jocks, sluts etc.). Moreover, *10 Things*, for all its formulaic predictability has retained much of the robustness and irreverence of the original (unlike another recent spin-off, Tommy O'Haver's *Get Over IT* (2001), an entirely forgettable high school comedy which feeds off Shakespeare's *A Midsummer Night's Dream*). Generic films set in the American high school experience allow for a wide range of variations, from George Lucas's memorable *American Graffiti* (1973) to Amy Heckerling's *Fast Times at Ridgemont High* (1982), with more 'serious' variations such as John Hughes' *The Breakfast Club* (1985), or nostalgic musical fantasies such as Randal Kleiser's *Grease* (1978). A high school romance/comedy contemporary with *10 Things*, Robert Iscove's *She's All That* (1999) develops the Pygmalion/Cinderella theme latent in *10 Things*, expressed through the miraculous transformation of a pretty, but geeky and bespectacled girl into a pretty, cool girl with 20/20 vision. Moving further afield, the family resemblances of *10 Things* stretch into teenage versions of literary classics in general, with Heckerling's *Clueless* (1995), based on Jane Austen's Emma, as a near relation and Roger Kumble's *Cruel Intentions* (1999), based on Choderlos de Laclos' 18th century novel *Les Liaisons Dangereuses*, and David Raynr's *Whatever it Takes* (2000), an adaptation of *Cyrano de Bergerac*, as more distant cousins.

Language and Portent: A Lightweight Moor?

Tim Blake Nelson's *O*, adapted for the screen by Brad Kayaa, was originally produced in 1999, but its release was delayed twice by Miramax, because of the tragic high school shootings at Columbine and at Santee high schools (Burt 2002). So from the outset the history of this film springs from an American saga of teenage violence. As with *10 Things*, the script is re-written in its entirety into modern American idiom. It is a high school version of Shakespeare's mature tragedy *Othello*, his only domestic tragedy. In the story Othello, the black general marries Desdemona, the white bourgeois Venetian girl, and subsequently is manipulated into jealous rage by his ensign, Iago, until he murders Desdemona. The entire play is dominated by the figure of Iago, a diabolical character who from the very beginning of the play announces his intention to the audience of bringing about the destruction of Othello.

Comedies of courtship, such as *The Taming of the Shrew* and *10 Things*, relate directly to the preoccupations of a teenage audience. Similarly, jealousy, and the interplay of male friendships and male-female relationships should translate fairly easily into an adolescent dating culture. And yet critics have found the murderous consequences of these jealousies in *O* unconvincing. Odin (Othello, played by Mehki Phifer) is the high school basketball star, and the only black boy in the preppy white school. Hugo (Iago, played by Josh Hartnett), a lower-ranking basketball player, is the son of the basketball coach and jealous of Odin's stardom and the attention given to Odin by his father. Desi (Desdemona, played by the ubiquitous Julia Stiles) is the popular and pretty daughter of the Dean. Hugo manipulates Odin into believing that Michael Casio, the second-best player on the baskeball team and envied by Hugo, is having an affair with Desi. Odin, with a record of drug abuse, gradually disintegrates, and ends up strangling Desi and committing suicide. Hugo, who has killed his co-conspirator Roger and wounded Michael Casio, is taken away by the police in the final scene. Three major organising ideas structure the film. One is the idea of having high school basketball as the competitive arena for the three major male characters, substituting for Shakespeare's military environment. Much has been made of this in the reviews; many critics feel that the world of basketball is inherently too trivial to be chosen as a setting for a Shakespearean tragedy (e.g., Elvis Mitchell's 'The Moor Shoots Hoops' 2001). The second organising idea is the introduction of the parental dimension, in particular the neglect that Hugo feels in relation to his father, the basketball coach (played with intensity by Martin Sheen) which gives Hugo a psychological motivation well-known from familial American drama, from Tennessee Williams, Eugene O'Neill and onwards, including echoes of James Dean's portrayal of Cal Trask in Elia Kazan's *East of Eden* (1954). This innovation in the script opens up the long critical discussion of the motivation – or lack of the same – of Iago, prompted by Coleridge's famous characterisation of Iago as a 'motiveless malignity in search of a motive' (1811-12) Is it possible to retain Iago/Hugo as the central diabolical driving force of the tragedy, if psychologically he is reduced to a poor kid yearning for the affection and attention of his father? The third organising idea is a metaphorical one thrust at the audience in the very first scene of the film: the dichotomous imagery of white doves and black hawks – the hawk being the symbol and mascot of the basketball team –with Hugo's voice over expressing his desire to be able to fly. This metaphorical frame simultaneously organises central themes in the film including the dichotomies of race, of competition and co-operation, and of savagery and gentleness. James M. Welsh, in his comparative study of *O* and Sax/Davies' television film *Othello* (2000), exemplifies classic critical reservations about 'teening Shakespeare' in his analysis: 'Kayaa somehow thought it might be a good idea to turn *Othello* into a backcourt tragedy, without realizing that a basketball star lacks the authority and tragic dimension of the Moor, elevated to a position of military leadership. Shooting hoops instead of Turks is less than a subtle difference' (2002, p.225). Welsh problematizes not only the change of setting, but also the loss of Shakespeare's language: '[C]an the high passions and extreme violence of the Shakespearean original survive a text that has not one whit of the original language? Language was the scaffolding upon which Shakespeare erected his improbable set of characters with their equally improbable motivations and behaviours. But without the glorious linguistic superstructure, can this pre-fab movie long endure?' (2002, p.225).

The answer to the second question must be that the key to making a film based on Shakespeare without the 'glorious linguistic superstructure' lies in creating a *cinematic equivalent* on a par with that language. Kurosawa, in his Japanese versions of *Macbeth* (*The Throne of Blood*, 1957) and *King Lear* (*Ran*, 1985) has done just that (not that I'm comparing Blake Nelson, as a director, to Kurosawa). The answer to the first question – whether the basketball court as a setting is *inherently* inimical to tragedy – surely must be that no setting *per se* is too trivial to encompass tragic action. By the same token, Rob Blackwelder's (2001) critique misses the point:

> [T]he key to 'Othello' is making the audience consider a guy who strangles his spouse out of jealousy to be a tragic figure. O doesn't accomplish that. Instead you wonder why Odin doesn't just break up with Desi and maybe sock her supposed lover in the kisser. I mean, it's high school. They've been dating four months. Let it go, man. There's plenty of fish in the sea.

I agree with Blackwelder's point that *O* is unsuccessful in developing Odin as a tragic protagonist. The implication in Blackwelder's critique, however, is that teenage relations are *inherently* incapable of functioning as a vehicle for tragedy. One refutation of this, of course, may be that Romeo and Juliet's relationship lasted less than four *days*! Another way of putting this problem into perspective may be to look at what is, in the view of most critics, a fairly successful 'teenage tragedy', Peter Weir's *Dead Poets' Society* (1989). In spite of its generic stereotypes of stuffy principals and parents versus young nonconformist teacher, of reducing literature to great quotes, and of toadies and rebels, it does construct a school environment and a set of characters whose conflicts and passions are convincing, and a suicide which makes dramatic sense within the parameters of the world of that film. The relative failure of *O* to persuade the audience of the dramatic inevitability of the tragic action stems not from the fact that we are dealing with teenage characters, nor from high school basketball being the arena of conflict. In my analysis, the hub around which *Othello* evolves is the intensity of the 'seduction' of Othello by Iago, the systematic brainwashing of Othello, and the single-mindedness of Iago. The sense of claustrophobia of that process is not achieved in *O* and consequently the audience is not gripped by the tragic inevitability of the outcome, but rather bemused and confused by the avalanche of violence.

Legacy Remediation in *Hamlet*

Michael Almereyda's *Hamlet* (2000) 🎬 in some ways may seem to stretch the definition of 'teenage Shakespeare'. Ethan Hawke (Hamlet) was 29 years old when the film was shot, and Almereyda, in several interviews, has disclaimed any targeting of a specifically teenage audience. There are however, a number of features about the film which place it in interesting parallel with *Romeo + Juliet*. Almereyda's *Hamlet* is a modern-dress version of the play, set in contemporary New York. Old Hamlet, 'King and CEO of the almighty Denmark Corporation', has died. Young Hamlet, wearing a knitted cap with ear flaps, is a computer and video freak who obsesses over old footage of his father and mother, and old movies. The use of striking settings is one of the characteristics of the film. Claudius, played slickly by Kyle Maclachlan of Twin Peaks fame, announces his takeover and his marriage to Gertrude (Diane Venora) at a press conference. The ghost of Hamlet's father first appears on security monitors inside the steel and glass palace of Denmark Corporation. Ophelia's madness scene is shot at a reception in the Guggenheim Museum. Hamlet's 'To be or not to be' soliloquy is in part shot in a Blockbuster video store. Claudius' 'chapel scene', in which he torments himself with guilt, is shot in a stretch limousine, with Hamlet driving, unknown to Claudius. The idea of placing *Hamlet* in a big business environment, however, was not Almereyda's. The Finnish director Aki Kaurismaki chose a similar environment for his black and white *Hamlet Goes Business* (1987), but the similarities end there. Whereas Kaurismaki's Business is a dead pan farce, with Hamlet as the mastermind of all the murders (but killed in the end by trade union rep Horatio!), *Hamlet*, like *Romeo + Juliet*, is a more 'faithful' attempt to construct contemporary cinematic strategies for Shakespeare's play. Like Luhrmann, Almereyda has kept and edited the original Shakespearean play text. But unlike Luhrmann's post-modernist theatricalities, Almereyda's *mise en scene* is a realistic representation of corporate New York, with subdued editing, and with dominating colours of greys and blacks creating a kind of neo-noir effect. It is in the representation of the character of Hamlet that Almereyda is breaking new ground. It is evident from the very first pictures of the film that the key to understanding Hamlet is in his absorption with media technologies. He constantly interacts, indeed represents himself, through his computer screen, or via a digital camera, and the digital editing of his own history, blending home video with a variety of film and television footage. His first version of the 'To be or not to be' soliloquy is a mix of himself on his computer screen; later we get the full version in the 'Action' aisle of a Blockbuster video store. The play in the play – 'the Mousetrap' – is a film edited by Hamlet, a grotesque collage of TV footage, old cinema and porn. Indeed, in the final dying scene, we get an inside view of Hamlet, represented in grainy pixels of black and white. Katherine Rowe, in her study '"Remember me": Technologies of Memory in Michael Almereyda's *Hamlet*" (2001) refers to what Peter Donaldson (2002) calls the 'media allegory' in Luhrmann's *Romeo + Juliet*, but, differs in her interpretation of this allegory:

> *The media allegory in Almereyda's* Hamlet *focuses more narrowly on technologies of memory. His preoccupation is the way film and video mediate past experience, both for the individual and the community. Yet Almereyda is more concerned than Luhrmann with the trade-offs these different technologies entail. For Almereyda's* Hamlet, *the personal video is the technology of interiority among a variety of modern media, including telephones, television, photography, film, and so on. All but one of Hamlet's soliloquies are framed as video sequences that he*

> has composed. As Hamlet dies, we see his life flash back in the same grainy black and white collage. ... Hamlet's videos create narratives of the past not for the purpose of accurate retrieval but in response to present interests and desires. The formal features of film and video supply a cognitive grammar for the mind as it stores and recombines the traces of the past. (p.6)

In concrete terms, these monologues of video collages, however interesting as devices and as metaphors of identity and memory retrieval, often appear without a strong organic connection to the scene. This is true of the 'Hecuba' speech ('O what a rogue and peasant slave am I') which is accompanied by footage of James Dean and John Gielgud among others. Connections are arguably there, but the collocation seems contrived. In addition to this, the strain of incorporating highly formalized Shakespearean blank verse (however heavily cut) into this high tech environment adds to the impression of a film with lots of ideas, but little to say about Shakespeare's story of Hamlet. In the final analysis, it is striking that, whereas Kaurismaki's *Hamlet Goes Business* in its own farcical way offered insightful comments on both Shakespeare's *Hamlet* and big business, and whereas Luhrmann's *Romeo + Juliet*, for all its post-modernist playfulness, presented a commentary on the *wasteland* of contemporary corporate culture and religiosity, Almereyda's *Hamlet* seems to have little or nothing to say about the corporate environment into which the story has been thrust.

Shakespeare: The 'Ageless Icon'

The four 'teened' Shakespeare films treated above form a perhaps too neat repertoire of teenage Shakespearean films: *10 Things I Hate About You* and *O* represent total revisions in modern idiom, set in teenage environments; *Romeo + Juliet* and Almereyda's *Hamlet* are attempts to retain Shakespeare's play text while creating broader contemporary, or near-contemporary settings chosen to inflect, illuminate and update Shakespeare's text. The inclusion of other examples, such as Haver's *Get Over It* (2001) or Billy Morrissette's *Scotland PA* (2002), a farcical spinoff of *Macbeth* set in the 1970s, would have given a more complete picture of the diversity of the field. Comparing the relative success or failure of these films is a bit like comparing apples and oranges. Luhrmann and Almereyda's films are big-budget movies with a corresponding range in terms of production values.

10 Things and *O*, by comparison, appear as shoe-string productions. Nevertheless, it is striking that the two plays with the strongest and most complex stories, *Hamlet* and *Othello*, have produced the least successful teenage versions. There is no simple explanation for this, but I'll venture one, anyway. The relative success of a film such as *10 Things* is carried by the director's and scriptwriter's sense of the *irreverence* of the original story. By the same token, the success of *Romeo + Juliet* is in great measure to be ascribed to Luhrmann's sense of the cinematic potential of near-future media-saturated corporate gangland warfare. *O*, postponed because of the Columbine and Santee shootings, had a vast potential for tapping into such themes as American sports hysteria, teenage violence, and race conflict, but seemed trapped between exploring these themes and developing the intensities of the plot. Almereyda's *Hamlet*, the most 'Shakespearean' of the four in the sense that this film has retained more of the original play text than the others, develops the idea of Hamlet's digital inwardness brilliantly, but has little to offer when it comes to the central organising themes of the play: Hamlet's madness, the Oedipal theme, and Hamlet's relation to the power games in the Denmark corporation. It is perhaps indicative of this film that the famous gravedigger scene is cut entirely. Almereyda has explained that 'it just didn't work'. I suggest that one of the reasons why it did not work was that the film, dominated by the sulking James Dean-like Ethan Hawke, was incapable of accommodating a humorous, philosophical Hamlet figure.

Richard Burt, one of the few critics who has engaged directly with the teenage Shakespeare film genre in his essay 'Afterword: Te(e)n Things I Hate' (2002a), uses the loaded term 'Shakesploitation' flicks. Rubricking *10 Things* with *Never Been Kissed* (1999), *Jawbreaker* (1999) and *The Rage – Carrie 2* (1999) among others, he is particularly concerned with what is in his view a problematic representation of gender. He asserts that the films:

> *[O]vertly thematize both the 'dumbing down' of Shakespeare seen in earlier high school movies such as* Porky's 2 *(dir. Bob Clark, 1986) and the figure of the loser that emerged in early nineties mass culture. Yet these newer films oppose female intelligence and loserdom so that Shakespeare literacy and receptivity by girls are allied with not smoking or drinking (drugs nearly go*

> *unmentioned), safe sex (both to prevent pregnancy and the transmission of STDs), waiting until you're ready for sex (not being a 'slut'), and so on.... This construction of female intelligence infantilizes rather than liberates teen girls, and one could rightly regard these extremely similar films as a conservative reaction to the more transgressive role pop stars like Madonna played in relation to teen girl wanna-bes in the 1980s with music videos like 'Express Yourself'. (Burt 2002a, pp.205-7)*

Burt's critique, published in *Spectacular Shakespeare* (2002) is just another instance of the complex ways in which the field of Shakespeare criticism interfaces with popular media culture in general, as well as with youth culture/youth cinema/high school movies, etc. The subdivisions of popular culture/youth culture are so manifold that whereas Burt's critique might, with some justification, be applied to comedies with a particular female focus such as *10 Things*, it is irrelevant in relation to *Romeo + Juliet*, as well as to *O* and Almereyda's *Hamlet*. As Gary Taylor has so amply documented in his monumental *Re-Inventing Shakespeare* (1991), there is no end to the use and abuse of Shakespeare, both as a storyteller and a cultural cachet. In that sense the history of Shakespearean film mirrors the performance history of Shakespeare's plays – indeed both are part of the broader history of re-inventing Shakespeare. In the 19th century Thomas Bowdler famously abridged and censored him and Charles and Mary Lamb turned him into stories for children; in the 1990s Hollywood teened him. The cultural history of re-inventing Shakespeare is a history of appropriation, because appropriating Shakespeare, in performance, on film, through novelization, in cartoons, and in criticism, is the only way to keep him alive. Shakespeare films targeting youthful audiences are neither better nor worse than other genres of appropriation, facing as they do the same kinds of creative dilemmas as any other genre of appropriation.

REFERENCES

Blackwelder, R. (2001) 'Hoops & Homicide', SPLICEDwire, URL (consulted May 2005): http://www.splicedonline.com/01reviews/o.html.

Boose, L.E. and R. Burt (eds.) (1997) *Shakespeare, the Movie: Popularizing the Plays on Film, Tv, and Video*. New York: Routledge.

Burnett, M.T. and R. Wray (eds.) (2000) *Shakespeare, Film, Fin de Siècle*. New York: St. Martin's Press.

Burt, R. (ed.) (2002) *Shakespeare After Mass Media*. New York: Palgrave.

Burt, R. (2002a) 'Afterword: Te(e)n Things I Hate about Girlene Shaksploitation Flicks in the Late 1990's, or Not-So-Fast Times at Shakespeare High', in C. Lehmann and L.S. Starks (eds.), *Spectacular Shakespeare: Critical Theory and Popular Cinema*, Madison, NJ: Fairleigh Dickinson University Press.

Donaldson, P. '"All Which It Inherit": Shakespeare's Globes and Global Media', *Shakespeare Survey*, 52: 183-200.

Donaldson, P. (2002) '"In Fair Verona": Media, Spectacle and Performance in William Shakespeare's Romeo + Juliet', in R. Burt (ed.), *Shakespeare After Mass Media*, Palgrave.

Frye N. (1957) *The Anatomy of Criticism: Four Essays*. Princeton, NJ: Princeton University Press.

Jerslev, A. (1992) 'Semiotics by Instinct: "Cult Film" as a Signifying Practice Between Audience and Film', in M. Skovmand and K. Shrøder (eds.) *Media Cultures: Reappraising Transnational Media*, pp.181-198. New York: Routledge.

Jerslev, A. (1999) 'Film Noir. Et netværk af familieligheder', *Kosmorama* 223: 4-28. *THIS IS

Lehmann, C. (2002) *Shakespeare Remains: Theater to Film, Early Modern to Postmodern*. Ithaca, NY: Cornell University Press.

Lehmann, C. and L.S. Starks (eds.) (2002) *Spectacular Shakespeare: Critical Theory and Popular Cinema*. Madison, NJ: Fairleigh Dickinson University Press.

Loehlin, J.N. (2000) '"These Violent Delights Have Violent Ends": Baz Luhrmann's Millennial Shakespeare', in M.T. Burnett and R. Wray (eds.) *Shakespeare, Film, Fin de Siècle*, pp.121-136. New York: St. Martin's Press.

Mitchell, E. (2001) 'The Moor Shoots Hoops', *New York Times* 31 August. *NOT SO SURE

Rowe, K. (2001) '"Remember Me": Technologies of Memory in Michael Almereyda's Hamlet', Bryn Mawr, PA: Bryn Mawr College Film Studies: Writing with Film, URL (consulted May 2005): http://www.brynmawr.edu/filmstudies/writing/professors/rowe1.html.

Taylor, G. (1991) *Re-inventing Shakespeare: A Cultural History from the Restoration to the Present*. New York: Oxford University Press.

Welsh, J. (2002) 'Classic Demolition: Why Shakespeare is Not Exactly "Our Contemporary", or "Dude, Where's My Hankie?"', *Literature Film Quarterly* 130(3): 223-227.

FILMS REFERENCED

Almereyda, M. (dir.) (2000) *Hamlet*. USA: Miramax Films.
Heckerling, A. (dir.) (1982) *Fast Times at Ridgemont High*. USA: Universal.
Heckerling, A. (dir.) (1995) *Clueless*. USA: Paramount.
Hughes, J. (dir.) (1985) *The Breakfast Club*. USA: Universal.
Iscove, R. (dir.) (1999) *She's All That*. USA: Miramax.
Junger, G. (dir.) (1999) *10 Things I Hate About You*. USA: Touchstone Pictures.
Kaurismäki, A. (dir.) (1987) *Hamlet Goes Business*. Finland: Villealfa Filmproductions.
Kazan, E. (dir.) (1954) *East of Eden*. USA: Warner Brothers.
Kleiser, R. (dir.) (1978) *Grease*. USA: Paramount.
Kumble, R. (dir.) (1999) *Cruel Intentions*. USA: Columbia Pictures.
Kurosawa, A. (dir.) (1957) *Throne of Blood*. Japan: Brandon Pictures.
Kurosawa, A. (dir.) (1985) *Ran*. Japan: Greenwich Film Production.
Lucas, G. (dir.) (1973) *American Graffiti*. USA: Universal.
Luhrmann, B. (dir.) (1992) *Strictly Ballroom*. Australia: Miramax Films.
Luhrmann, B. (dir.) (1996) *Romeo + Juliet*. USA: Twentieth Century Fox.
Luhrmann, B. (dir.) (2001) *Moulin Rouge!* USA: Bazmark Films.
Morrissette, B. (dir.) (2002) *Scotland, PA*. USA: Abandon Pictures.
Nelson, T.B. (dir.) (2001) *O*. USA: Daniel Fried Productions.
Nichols, M. (dir.) (1967) *The Graduate*. USA: Embassy Pictures.
O'Haver, T. (dir.) (2001) *Get Over It*. USA: Miramax.
Raynr, D. (dir.) (2000) *Whatever It Takes*. USA: Phoenix Pictures.
Weir, P. (dir.) (1989) *Dead Poet's Society*. USA: Touchstone Pictures.
Wise, R. and J. Robbins (dirs.) (1961) *West Side Story*. USA: United Artists.
Zeffirelli, F. (dir.) (1968) *Romeo and Juliet*. UK: Paramount.

Index

10 Things I Hate About You: 157, 160-162, 167-169
aesthetic device: 110
adaptation: 12-20, 23, 26-27, 29, 32, 35-38, 40, 46-47, 50, 53, 55-57, 59, 61-62, 64, 66-68, 71, 73-74, 82, 85, 94, 98, 100, 103-105, 112, 114, 117, 125-126, 128-130, 139-145, 147, 149-154, 162
Adaptation: 59-61, 64-65, 68, 71, 74-75
Adorno, Theodor: 99
American Graffiti: 162
anime: 19, 23-27, 29-30
appropriation: 26, 38, 157, 169
archetypes: 37, 45, 47,
Austen, Jane: 128, 162
authorization: 99
avant-garde: 80, 84, 97, 113
avatar: 26, 50-53
Axel, Gabriel: 117, 126-131, 133
Babette's Feast: 19, 117, 122-123, 125-130, 133-135
Barthes, Roland: 81, 154
basketball: 163-165
Being John Malkovich: 60, 74
Blackadder's Christmas Carol: 150-151
Black & White: 37
blank verse: 159, 167
Blixen, Karen: 19, 117-122, 125-126, 128, 130, 133
Bowdler, Thomas: 169
The Breakfast Club: 162
Breaking the Waves: 107, 109, 114
Burroughs, William: 82
Campbell, Joseph: 45
Casablanca: 75
A Christmas Carol: 18, 141, 144, 149-152
cinematic environment: 40
cinematic mediation: 110
cinematographe: 11

Clueless: 162
comedy: 127-128, 160-162
comics: 16, 20, 37, 41-46, 48-49, 56
comics, superhero: 37, 42-43, 45-46
communities of content: 25
convergence: 56
credits: 61, 63-66, 74, 130
cross-filming: 127-128
Cruel Intentions: 162
Cunningham, Michael: 86-90, 92-94
Dancer in the Dark: 107, 114
Dead Poets' Society: 165
Dean, James: 159, 163, 167-168
descriptive pause: 84
deus ex machina: 65-66, 76, 104
Dickens, Charles: 18-19, 139, 141-154
diegesis: 65, 108-110
diegetic: 42, 62-66, 69, 73
Dinesen, Isak: 117-118, 121, 126
domestic-universal combination strategy: 19, 117, 120, 128, 133-135
doujinshi: 30, 32
Dreyer, Carl Th.: 98, 100, 103-104, 113-114
dual orientation: 117, 120, 127-128
East of Eden: 163
Eisenstein, Sergei: 144-145
emotional insistency: 84
emotions: 19, 79, 81-84, 88, 94, 122, 141
Empire: 84
enunciation: 79, 113
Epidemic: 109
Euripides: 98-101, 103-106, 112-114
Europa: 109-110
fabula: 111-112
fantasy: 28, 49, 54, 160
Fast Times at Ridgemont High: 162
Final Fantasy: 42, 54-55
flashback: 69, 75, 144
A Flintstones Christmas Carol: 152

folktale motifs: 153
Family Guy: 19, 140-141, 145, 152
Frye, Northrop: 161
Futurama: 19, 141, 145, 152
games, computer: 31, 36, 40, 41, 42, 47, 50-53, 57
games, role-playing: 54
games, video: 16, 18, 35, 37, 40, 46-49, 54-57
Genette, Gerard: 14, 60-61, 79-81, 112
genre: 20, 23, 43, 59-62, 64, 68, 72-73
Get Over It: 162, 167
Grease: 162,
Great Expectations: 18, 146-149
Griffith, D.W.: 144-145
gumi: 31
Hamlet: 157, 165-169
heritage films: 129, 133
heteroglossia: 145-146
high school movies: 161, 168-169
Hollywoodification: 70
Hong Kong cinema: 52
The Hours: 19, 79, 84-85
HULK: 37, 42, 56
human-computer interaction: 47
hypermediacy: 15, 18, 29, 39-40, 51, 54, 56
hyperreal: 14-15, 54
hypertext: 14-15, 18, 47
The Idiots: 107, 114
immediacy: 15, 18, 29, 39-40, 54
inner monologue: 91
interactivity: 47, 55
intertextuality: 39, 54, 60-61, 93, 158
invisible art: 45
Jackson, Peter: 48, 55
Jolie, Angelina: 51
Jonze, Spike: 20, 59, 62, 65
joypad: 53
Kaufman, Charlie: 59-60, 62-76
Kaurismaki, Aki: 166-167
The Kingdom: 110
Kurosawa, Akira: 164
Künstlerroman: 60
La Jeteé: 82
Lamb, Charles and Mary: 169
The League of Extraordinary Gentlemen: 37, 46

Les Liaisons Dangereuses: 162
Lord of the Rings: 12, 40, 55, 82
Love's Labours' Lost: 161
Lumiere, Auguste: 11, 20
Lumiere, Louis Jean: 11, 20
manga: 26-27, 30, 32
McLuhan, Marshall: 38-39
Medea: 97-108, 112-114
megatext: 59, 61, 72-73
Melies, George: 11, 20
melodrama: 83, 149
The Merchant of Venice: 161
metafiction: 60, 65, 91-94, 147, 149-151
metafilm: 59-60, 64
Mickey's Christmas Carol: 151
A Midsummer Night's Dream: 162
Moulin Rouge!: 159
Mr. Magoo's Christmas Carol: 151-152
MTV: 46, 158
multimedia: 20, 23, 26, 29, 32, 35
The Muppet Christmas Carol: 150-151
Myst: 37
narration, causal: 41
narration, sequential: 41
narratives, unblocked: 82-84
narrator: 67, 79-81, 107-108, 110-113, 130, 134, 147, 150
narrator, implied: 80, 110
novelization: 169
O: 157, 162-165, 167-169
oekaki: 32
Oliver Twist: 18, 139-147, 149, 153
Orlean, Susan: 59, 61-71, 73, 75
Othello: 162-165, 168
Out of Africa: 121, 126, 130, 133-135
PAC-MAN: 50
palimpsest: 19, 61, 64, 66, 75
paraphrase: 67, 99
paratexts: 60-61, 149, 151, 153
The Passion of Joan of Arc: 103-104, 114
Ran: 164
rearticulation: 12
Rebel Without a Cause: 159
remediation: 12, 14-20, 28, 35, 37-40, 45, 47, 50, 54, 56, 61, 97, 114

repurposing: 12-13, 16, 18
Resident Evil: 37, 52-53, 55
romance: 28, 30, 147, 160-162
Romeo and Juliet: 157-159, 164
Russian formalism: 36
science fiction: 27, 29, 49, 54, 139, 149
Scotland PA: 167
Scrooge: 18, 149-152
Seven Gothic Tales: 118-119, 121
Shakespeare, William: 19, 75, 84, 157-169
Shakesploitation: 168
She's All That: 162
sign systems: 111
South Park: 146-147, 149, 152
split narrative: 107
steam punk: 54
Streep, Meryl: 70, 126
syuzhet: 111
The Taming of the Shrew: 160, 162
teening: 157, 160, 164
telefilm: 19, 97
textuality: 63, 150
thriller: 61, 72-73, 81-82
The Throne of Blood: 164
Tolkien, J.R.R: 55
Tomb Raider: 37, 50-52
translation: 16, 36, 53, 99, 111, 122, 134
transmission: 99, 169
transparency: 14-15, 18, 40, 98
Trier, Lars von: 19, 97-100, 103-110, 112-114
A Trip to the Moon: 11
underground comics: 43
Verfremdungseffect: 142, 150
video games: 16, 18, 35, 37, 40, 47-49, 54-55, 57
voice over: 63, 66, 69-70, 76, 90, 107, 110, 130, 142-143, 147, 163
Warhol, Andy: 84
Waugh, Patricia: 60, 65
Welles, Orson: 125-126
West Side Story: 159
William Shakespeare's Romeo + Juliet: 157- 159, 165-169
window: 13-15, 17-20, 29-30, 39, 69, 83, 88, 92, 111, 148
Wishbone: 141-143, 145, 152

Woolf, Virginia: 91-94
The X-Files: 149-150, 152
X-Men: 37, 45-46